To A

A go...

one of the few

who might actually

understand it

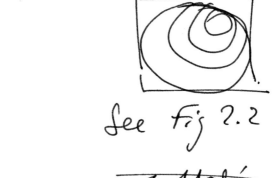

See Fig 2.2

From Concepts to Capabilities

From Concepts to Capabilities

Understanding and Exploiting Change as a Competitive Advantage

Jacques A.G. Halé

JOHN WILEY & SONS

Chichester . New York . Brisbane . Toronto . Singapore

Other Wiley Editorial Offices

John Wiley & Sons, Inc., 605 Third Avenue,
New York, NY 10158–0012, USA

Jacaranda Wiley Ltd, 33 Park Road, Milton,
Queensland 4064, Australia

John Wiley & Sons (Canada) Ltd, 22 Worcester Road,
Rexdale, Ontario M9W 1L1, Canada

John Wiley & Sons (SEA) Pte Ltd, 37 Jalan Pemimpin #05–04,
Block B, Union Industrial Building, Singapore 2057

ISBN 0-471-95798-4

Typeset by the author in Times New Roman
using Microsoft Word for Windows™ 6.0. in 10/12pt
Printed and bound in Great Britain by Bookcraft (Bath) Ltd,
This book is printed on acid-free paper responsibly manufactured from sustainable forestation,
for which at least two trees are planted for each one used for paper production.

To
my Parents Martial and Odette
who gave me life, love and much more

Contents

—— Acknowledgements

The material of this book has been accumulated over several decades of scientific, engineering, managerial and consultancy activities and experiences. Each contact with a skilled manager or technician was a source of inspiration. But the single individual who has influenced me most is without doubt John C. Edwards, the founder of ADT (Associative Design Technology) in Westborough (Mass). A brilliant mathematician, philosopher and computer scientist, he unified the fields of information science and systems into a coherent vision of the underlying principles of organisations. I hope that I have not betrayed too much the clarity and power of his analysis.

Two individuals who helped me realise the importance of some 'non-technical' concepts in organisations are Tom Gilb and Larry Phillips. Tom has been writing for the computer community for a long time — on what is quality, how to measure it, how to negotiate it — and his message is always as clear as it was in his first publication. The notion of capability which is central to this book is the result of his teaching. Dr Larry Philips is teaching and practising decision analysis at the London School of Economics. Although from a different perspective, Larry's views were helpful in getting at the concepts underlying the working of an organisation.

The events which led me to put together what I had accumulated throughout the years are the responsibility of David O'Brien. During his turn of office as Chief Executive of National & Provincial Building Society, a leading British financial institution, he had the intellectual courage to challenge the traditional ways of running a business, and his vision induced a different mode of being for the whole organisation. The clarity of his thinking is an inspiration.

I am also grateful to my colleagues at the now defunct VSF Limited who have directly contributed to enhance and test many of the techniques described in this book. Dr George Bricker, in particular, with his formidable conceptual creativity, helped to solidify some of the more elusive aspects of the approach. I am also grateful to Chris Craig-Jones and Mark Parnaby who validated and improved the techniques and the tools in actual business situations.

Malcolm Peltu, currently a free-lance journalist, helped me greatly with his vast culture in the field, doing a thorough editing job on the manuscript.

There are many others to whom I owe a great deal of support and encouragement. I am deeply indebted to all of them but especially to the closest one, Carole, my enduring partner in life and business.

Preface

The subject of business processes has received an exceptional level of attention during the 1990s, although the subject is not new — after all, the pioneering studies of Adam Smith and Frederick Taylor in the last century were all about equivalent industrial processes. However, there is a sense that a fresh way of looking at business, industry, administrations and services is now desirable and even critical for the survival of most organisations. The severe economic recessions of the 1980s brought home to every individual the truth that the old way of doing things is not always the best one. The need for a new vision is clear and is articulated by a number of visionary thinkers: Alvin Toffler and Charles Handy provide us with some pointers on where society as a whole is going. Edward de Bono shows us the power of creative thinking and the value of concepts in all aspects of business and services. Michael Hammer, James Champy and Richard Pascale — to quote only a few of the most influential management thinkers — force us to question the established ways in business.

This book is for those who are convinced that the world is not going to stop changing and that a bit of method and a set of techniques could be instrumental in controlling the boat. Management dates back centuries but has often been considered more an art than a science. I hope, however, that the skill and intuition of good managers can be complemented with a systematic understanding of the generic mechanisms behind organisations, so that sustainable business processes can be designed and operated.

My ambition in writing this book is not to explore the vision of the future but to take an engineering perspective of the world of organisations, in order to find a systematic approach to get from here to the vision so eloquently described by others. It therefore describes an approach for managers and business analysts involved in initiating and steering changes in their organisation. The challenge is to answer the question: 'Is there a way to decompose the "Big Bang" of change, advocated by some, into its atomic steps which can be understood and mastered by those who are responsible for these major changes?'

I feel necessary, for the sake of consistency, to define some common terms (such as process, resources, capability, concepts, value, events) in the context of process design. I hope that the reader will accept these conventions as a way of documenting the approach. Sitting for the first time in a small sailing boat or a light aircraft might trigger some dark panic when the craft is tossed about by the elements. But when it is possible to name and distinguish the rolling from the pitching, we may feel that there is some method after all in the madness of the situation.

The book is set out in five parts as follows:

- Part I introduces the main questions facing those responsible for business processes. Why design or redesign the processes of an organisation? Are there different levels of concerns? Are there different approaches?

- Part II outlines a philosophy of the control of change and a method for the design of business processes as a series of managed steps.

- Part III is the most formal and describes a method for the analysis and design of processes based on the notion of value.

- Part IV brings all the results of analysis and design together for the planning of the physical resources which will be implemented in the actual organisation

- Part V gathers reference information about the aBCd™ method and the terms used throughout the book.

The diagram below gives the linkage between the various chapters. A continuous thread runs through most of the chapters but two of them deal with self-standing subjects: Chapter 2 is an introduction to a process maturity model and Chapter 6 shows how to design a generic management architecture.

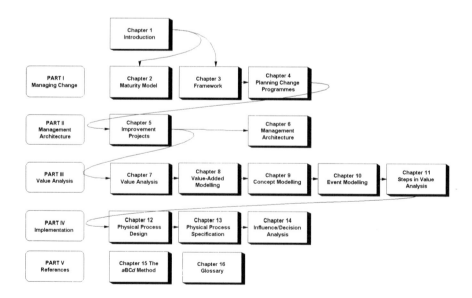

Overview of the Book

Compiling this book was a task vulnerable to errors and confusion. I would appreciate your feedback for future editions. Comments, corrections and suggestions should be sent to the author care of John Willey & Sons, Baffins Lane, Chichester, PO19 1UD, UK, or by electronic mail to 100112,1272 (Compuserve) or 100112.1272@compuserve.com.

Chapter 1

Introduction

BACKGROUND

The Scientific Organisation of Work

The history of management has a parallel with the history of industry. Before the industrial revolution, work was organised by the position that people had in life. It was clear what people were doing from their profession: baker, cobbler, farm hand, bailiff, squire.

The industrial revolution brought about the need to define 'jobs' and the 'scientific organisation of work' which was first done coherently by Adam Smith as early as 1776 and later on by Frederick Taylor. This led to a type of organisation similar to a classic military structure, where work is divided up according to standardised actions for manufacturing standardised parts. The detailed decomposition of the tasks was well documented into a hierarchy.

Taylorism is the name given to this approach to 'scientific management'. It aims for high efficiency through a better use of the human resources — but this is difficult to achieve without rigid rules of control and discipline. An exclusive concern for efficiency leads quickly to economies of scale that encourage the building of larger and larger organisations. The penalty is the decomposition of the functions into departments, deskilling, dehumanisation of work and lack of motivation. The scientific organisation of work also concentrates the attention onto the internal workings of the organisation, where customer and market remain 'outside' concerns.

The result is an *efficient* but highly *ineffective* organisation delivering the mass services and products required by the market, but failing to deliver quality services and products. Progressive paralysis becomes apparent when the economic environment becomes less tolerant to less competitive services or products. And as world competition becomes more open, the shift of the market from seller to buyers, the demise of some giant international corporations and growing importance of Information Technology (IT) are forcing new relationships with all stakeholders.

The 'second industrial revolution' or *information revolution*, brought about by IT, made matters worse by automating ineffective practices and allowed universal access to information. Because control is based on information, this challenged the strict hierarchy of management.

The reality of most large organisations has evolved a mixture of practice and technology from all the past ages, the 'rural', the 'industrial' and the 'information' ages, as described in the case of a modern army by Edward Guthrie, technical advisor to the Chief of Staff of the US Army (Guthrie 1994).

The Age of BPR

During the 1990s an attempt has been made to recover a holistic view of work through the management of the outcome rather than the activities. This requires that we understand the processes running through the functions of the organisation. These functions have tended to evolve as independent entities. The notion of 'internal customer', introduced as a way of restoring quality, actually reinforced this view of isolated functions, dealing with each other rather than with the ultimate customer (see Figure 1.1). This questioning of the organisation as a set of isolated functions started in the field of manufacture with the pioneering work of Edward Deming in the 1960s (Deming 1986) and is now applied to other industries and services. Deming advocated a system view of interdependent processes.

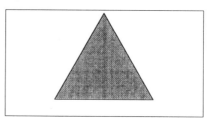

the organisation as it is described

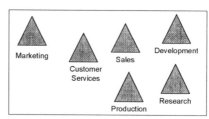

the organisation as it is in reality

Figure 1.1 The Isolated Functions

The shift to a new way of looking at organisations was stimulated largely by a seminal article in 1990 by Michael Hammer in which he argued the case behind his now famous saying 'Do Not Automate, Obliterate!' (Hammer 1990). This triggered a movement described as a new discipline, Business Process Re-Engineering. Although this is sometimes viewed with suspicion as a new management fashion, it is a powerful challenge to established practices and is here to stay. It has been described in a somewhat esoteric manner as a 'paradigm shift', simply meaning a fresh way of looking at organisations in all their aspects. What Michael Hammer advocates is a 'Big Bang' approach, starting from scratch, questioning the purpose of the organisation, its customer's needs, its relationship with its customer and its functioning.

This is consistent with a complete shift in the way of thinking but is not always helpful when it comes to deciding what to do next. What is needed is not necessarily a big explosion but a series of small explosions similar to those in an internal combustion engine, producing movement without destruction. In other words, in order to build a new organisation to replace the one which has just been 'obliterated', the revolutionaries need to become engineers. Yet in a survey in 1994 of companies in the UK, 83% of corporate executives said they believed the pace of change was increasing rapidly, but only 8% said they have a formal change management structure in place (Hutton 1994 with kind permission of Proudfoot Creative Services Ltd).

MANAGING CHANGE

Change has become a fact of life for everyone in an organisation and especially for managers. Change should therefore not be seen as an exceptional happening requiring special measures, but should be a normal component of everyday activities.

The Challenges

Organisations having to cope with dramatic changes are forced to question the basic assumptions of business and public service. They have to cope with a more complex work environment; devolve decision taking; take account of the need for empowerment and team working and look at work through roles rather than jobs. This can be unsettling for people used to well-structured jobs.

The challenge is to design an organisation which is at the same time flexible to long-term changes in the economical and cultural environments and resilient to immediate threats. This is similar to designing ships which must be capable of coping with different missions and of resisting severe weather and tide conditions.

The objectives for redesigning the processes of an organisation should include:

- 'dramatic' performance improvements;
- improve process effectiveness first, then process efficiency;

- quality control embedded in the processes.

According to James Champy, more than two thirds of US and European companies are involved in some kind of re-engineering projects (Champy 1995). In the early 1990s, most projects resulted from crisis situations and were aimed at cost-cutting. In the mid-1990s, these projects are undertaken more by ambition than survival and are more likely to succeed more efficient processes.

Labour reduction is often the justification for BPR and has given a bad press to the movement. This is a confusion in the order of the objectives. Waste reduction and removing 'non-added values' activities are necessary. This often means wholesale reduction of staff in the short term. But organisations which do not try to be more effective before being more efficient, do not build for the future and could end up with a crippled organisation — more efficient but no better equipped to compete.

The Methods

Management is based on the manipulation of concepts, on the translation of ideas into physical reality. Alvin Toffler in his seminal books, such as *Future Shock* or *The Third Wave*, describes the coming of the age of information where management as a discipline has to evolve from an art into an engineering discipline (Toffler 1970 and 1980). This demands better attitudes and skills than 'flying by the seat of the pants'. As in any engineering discipline, in addition to intuition and experience, we need a foundation theory; applied theories; intellectual techniques and tools; means of measuring; reference databases; education (in the concepts) and training (in the techniques and tools).

In spite of the comings and going of fads, there is an underlying increase in the sophistication of the management techniques in the area which concerns us in this book — the design, or redesign, of organisation, management and processes. Richard Pascale, the international expert on management, compiled a history of recent managerial ideas, neatly presented in one of his diagrams as a kind of geological build-up of strata of ideas (Pascale 1990). Each successive idea contributes to raise the collective understanding of the domain, even if its contribution becomes buried by new ideas.

In this book we shall try to dig down to the bedrock — to use the geological analogy of Richard Pascale — for a more stable foundation upon which the valid ideas of the past and present can be repositioned. We shall concentrate on the theory and the techniques for designing better processes.

WHAT IS BUSINESS PROCESS ENGINEERING?

Different organisations are at different stages of understanding the challenges, which sometimes contributes to confusion about what BPR is meant to be. I shall examine, in the next chapter, a model of process maturity which will help us to decide the appropriate techniques in each case.

I believe the following definition proposed by Joe Peppard and Philip Rowland does provide a common ground, which I will adopt in this book:

'BPR is an improvement philosophy. It aims to achieve step improvements in performance by redesigning the processes through which an organisation operates, maximising their value-added contents and minimising everything else. This approach can be applied at an individual level or to the whole organisation' (Peppard and Rowland 1995).

In broad terms, there are four main motivations for reviewing and redesigning processes:

1) *Business Re-Engineering (BR)*: challenging the purpose, customer needs and position of the whole organisation;

2) *Business Process Re-Engineering (BPR)*: challenging an area of the business;

3) *Process Improvement*: challenging the efficiency of the activities;

4) *IT Repositioning*: challenging the way technology — especially IT — contributes to the goals of the organisation as a resource in the processes.

Motivations for Business Process Re-Engineering Projects

The difference in motivation is indicated by the origin of the person or team asking the questions, as summarised in Figure 1.2 and the following text.

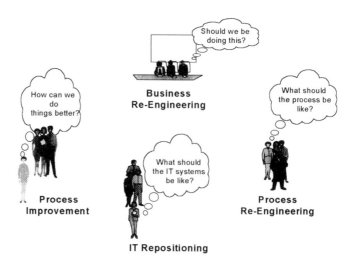

Figure 1.2 Four Motivations for Redesigning Processes

Business Re-Engineering:

If the concern comes from Senior Management, such as a Board, Executive Committee or Vice-President, the questions are likely to be of the kind: *'Are we in the right business?'*, *'What is our business about'*. It is this set of concerns which requires a radical rethinking of the organisation, as advocated by Michael Hammer, leading to dramatic changes at all levels, including the basic aims and functioning of the enterprise.

Process Re-Engineering:

When the initiative comes from a manager in charge of a department or a function such as customer services, IT or manufacture, the questioning is often limited to challenging the way that department or function delivers its contribution to the organisation's objectives — which is not what the business is about. *The challenge is about the way the processes are designed.* Experience shows that it is very difficult to influence upwards. The Board may be impressed by the initiative but will not automatically question their own constituency.

Process Improvement:

The third type of initiative is the 'traditional' process improvement: the process is not challenged in its design but in *the way it is implemented,* the aim being to improve its efficiency. This is the traditional ambition of quality improvement, Quality Circles and Total Quality Management (TQM) programmes which have been undertaken since the 1960s.

IT Repositioning

The fourth type of situation is concerned with IT. The IT (or IS) department could benefit from BPR like any other function. But there is also a communication problem in developing specifications, caused by the culture gap between the IT community and the executives of the organisation. The two-way dialogue must be repaired. What is needed is a repositioning of the IT function in the organisation, breaking the isolation of the IT specialists. The challenge for IT specialists is to sell their competence — systematic and analytical thinking, technical expertise and knowledge of the technology — and to acquire more sensitivity to the goals of the organisation in delivering its mission. But on the other hand, there is also a responsibility for the executives to express what they want in terms which can be implemented. The solution to these problems requires co-operation between both parties, in which a facilitator (internal or external) is often required. A common way of describing processes would also be an advantage.

THE NEED FOR A HOLISTIC SET OF METHODS, TECHNIQUES AND TOOLS

A holistic re-engineering approach should provide the tools for different types of needs (see Figure 1.3). This should offer an easy method to define the vision. Then the vision should be documented in a way which can be exploited further for defining the core capabilities These core capabilities will define the core processes. Re-engineering should then be concerned with aligning the existing organisation to the core processes by specifying the required people and systems capabilities. The scope of re-engineering could be restricted to some of the more critical processes or could encompass all the processes.

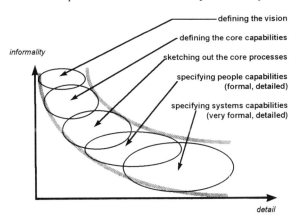

Figure 1.3 Scope of Holistic BPR Techniques

The closer to implementation, the more formal and detailed the techniques need to be. Informal techniques are used to sketch out the new processes, but the definition of the requirements of the people and the systems capabilities need to be more formal and precise. Also, automated tools and design workbenches become more and more necessary as the need for formality, consistency and detail increases towards the implementation of the processes.

Radical and Continuous Improvements

A re-engineering programme is a series of radical changes and continuous quality improvement (see Figure 1.4).

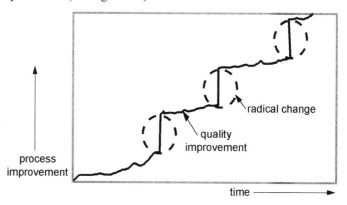

Figure 1.4 Radical and Continuous Improvements

Historically, periods of great changes are followed by periods of consolidation, revolutions are followed by periods of stability (and often prosperity). In Part I, we shall review an organisation of change consistent with this philosophy.

The Sigmoid Curve

When is it appropriate to have a radical change? Charles Handy proposes a way to build a new future while maintaining the present (Handy 1994). He calls it the 'Pathway through Paradox' and illustrates it with the so-called 'Sigmoid Curve', illustrated on Figure 1.5. The term 'sigmoid' is a reference to the shape of the curve, 'like an S shape'. This curve expressed the life of many things but in particular empires, organisations and products. We often use the term 'life-cycle' although it is not actually a cycle but a rise and fall. This illustrates that human endeavours grow from humble beginnings, prosper and eventually fall, if not properly looked after. The secret of constant growth is to start a new Sigmoid Curve before the first one collapses.

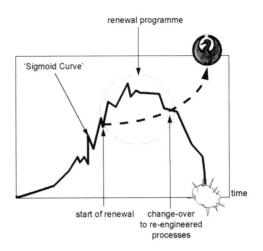

Figure 1.5 The 'Sigmoid Curves' of an Organisation

In the context of BPR, this means that it is when the going is good (the fast rising part of the curve) that we should start thinking about the next radical change. This is best initiated as an 'off-line' project. By the time the existing activities run out of steam and the going gets tough, then we have an alternative in the wing ready to take over for a radical renewal. It is a reflection of the quality of their management that the best run organisations are those which continuously question the way they are run. The best advertised example is probably Motorola which still achieved a growth rate of 20% in 1994, in spite of a generally depressed economy. The terms that Motorola use are indicative of this pioneering spirit: *'Our challenge is to drive our vision beyond everyone's expectation, (our tactic) is to develop organisational iconoclasts'* (Canavan 1994).

In Part I, I shall suggest ways to rationalise the renewal 'change' programme shown on Figure 1.5.

THE CULTURAL DIMENSION: THE ROLE OF MANAGEMENT

There are hidden consequences of re-engineering an organisation. The traditional hierarchy inherited from the industrial revolution is not well suited to the new challenges of better delivery of service or products. A new management culture is soon required which would encourage and support decentralisation. This is compounded with the technical availability of information at all levels.

Hierarchy

The picture is not black and white: the 'bad' hierarchy and the 'good' decentralisation. A strict hierarchical management structure has some positive consequences. For example, it can provide a sense of individual security; give some guarantee of predictable outcome; create a uniformity of image and interaction with the 'outside world'; and deliver a good control over existing resources.

But there are also negative aspects of a strict hierarchical structure which are being highlighted increasingly. The structure is slow to react to changes and to evolve; it leads to heavy bureaucracy for the procurement of new resources; it is demotivating for those who could best contribute; it encourages a general reluctance to admit and discuss inevitable problems; and it can generate distrust at all levels.

A number of changes in the culture and the functioning of the new style of organisation have become necessary. These are consistent with those seen elsewhere in society and business, such as:

- re-enforcement of the customer requirements as the justification for the organisation;
- the need to redefine the processes delivering the services and products to customers;
- implementation of an organisation around the processes which deliver the services;
- working in operational teams which have all the skills required for the defined processes;
- support to the operational teams by clear management of direction and capabilities;
- devolution of decision making to the teams — 'subsidiarity' or 'federalism'.

Subsidiarity

The concept of 'subsidiarity' illustrates the culture usually associated with process re-engineering. It is discussed by Charles Handy in the seminal book *The Empty Raincoat* (Handy 1994), who defines it as the '*localisation of the decisions at the point closest to the delivery of the services or products*'. Subsidiarity is not a pretty word but it describes a simple idealised concept - a management approach where decisions are made at the lowest level possible.

Within the notion of subsidiarity, the central headquarters (HQ) sets policy and standards but does not necessarily specify how the services or products should be delivered. Subsidiarity requires smaller units, which support other units and the organisation as a whole.

The HQ should not claim for itself functions which can be performed by smaller/local bodies. The centre *empowers* the smaller units and tolerates individuality in meeting local needs. The consequence is a flatter organisation. The small units *delegate upwards* some responsibilities to the HQ, for resources, guidance, consistency between units and outside representation. The HQ should influence the activities of the smaller units but should only intervene or even interfere in order to avoid crisis.

The Roles of Senior Managers

The centre carries the ultimate responsibility for the whole organisation and acts as trustee of the future. Its role is to lock together the individual units (teams) — making co-operation between the teams effective and ensuring there is a consistent interface with the other stakeholders.

The role of 'chairman' or 'chief executive' should be to ensure that the direction of the organisation is properly addressed. The role has the ultimate responsibility for the process of transformation, ensuring that transformations are initiated, facilitated, sustained and understood by all the stakeholders.

The role of manager is key to the success of the transition. There are many challenges for managers. They have to change their style from control to facilitation. They have to be role models for the new culture through encouragement, coaching, support, empowerment, supervision without control. They have the responsibility for clarifying and communicating the mission, the goals and the policy. And they have to balance many conflicting requirements in order to bring about the necessary changes.

This is not pure philosophy but a deep cultural component of re-engineering which must be understood. The degree of acceptance of the consequences of 'subsidiarity' will determine the degree of radicalism of the change programme. Some organisations are better positioned than others to undertake radical changes. We shall review in Part I a model of process maturity which can be used to document the feasibility of particular changes.

CONCLUSIONS

I believe the way of thinking associated with BPR is here to stay and is an enrichment of the skills of managers. What is now needed is an approach to translate this change of thinking into implementable results. In the coming chapters, we shall review practical methods and techniques for tackling the organisation and running of change programmes along this new line of thinking.

Part I
Managing Change

Chapter 2

A Process Maturity Model

INTRODUCTION

The way processes are implemented in a given organisation can vary widely, from formal computer-based automation to simple informal procedures passed on from person to person. Faced with the need for inevitable changes, a given organisation will react in different manners according to its level on a *process maturity* scale. The techniques used to design, manage and improve these processes also covers a wide spectrum. A given technique can be too simplistic or too complicated for the requirements of a particular organisation.

Recognising the level of process maturity of an organisation can be helpful in recommending which particular process improvement approach is appropriate. This chapter introduces a simple but effective model for determining the maturity of an organisation and for understanding the approach needed for improving or redesigning its processes. This combines ideas which have been developed in both organisational and software disciplines.

INDIVIDUAL MODES OF WORKING

The process maturity of an organisation characterises the quality of its processes and its ability to understand and anticipate changes in the way it operates. It is influenced by the way in which its business processes are implemented and managed as well as by the abilities of its leaders and the time horizon that they can cope with.

Elliott Jaques of the Tavistock Institute of Human Relations and Institute of Organisation and Social Studies at Brunel University, has proposed a useful framework for understanding the various levels of concrete and abstract capabilities in people and how they relate to organisational functions (Jaques 1976 and Jaques, Gibson & Issac 1978).

Jaques defined five main levels of work, each of which can be characterised by the thinking and activities of a certain type of knowledge. These are:

1) the 'proceduralist' or 'pragmatic specialist: competent, persistent and attentive to detail;

2) the 'practitioners' or 'pragmatic generalists': good at organising their own work and that of others;

3) the 'system-setters' or 'theoretical generalists': good at gathering and organising quantities of information; using other people constructively; creating a context in which others can work; operating across a wide field; and having a good planning ability;

4) the 'structuralists' or 'theoretical specialists': intellectually very able, subtle, creative and very self-contained in their work, towards which they take an essentially theoretical approach (typically researchers and consultants);

5) the 'originators': usually take an original approach to a problem even when this may not be appropriate.

In practice, a given individual will be able to operate in different modes and will mix these different approaches in the same work. However, there is also a 'ceiling' for each individual.

The stratification of the capabilities of individuals with respect to abstraction seems to be reflected in the work content as well. The scope of the work of an organisation can be similarly described with similar concepts:

1) *prescribed action*: executing the instructions in hand;

2) *prescribed output*: working towards objectives which can be specified beforehand, according to defined circumstances;

3) *situational response*: carrying out work where the precise objectives to be pursued have been judged according to the needs of each specific concrete situation;

4) *systematic service provision*: making systematic provision of services of some given kinds shaped to the needs of a continuous sequence of concrete situations;

5) *comprehensive service provision*: making comprehensive provision of particular services according to the total and continuing needs for them throughout some given territorial or organisational society;

6) *comprehensive field coverage*: providing comprehensive services within some general field of need throughout some given territorial or organisational society;

7) *environment influence*: contributing to change the technological or the relational framework of economy and society.

GROUP MODES OF WORKING

The time horizon of a process or organisation relates closely with the span of its considerations — its 'business horizon' — and its relation to other processes or businesses. By extending his observations of the work of individuals to the organisation of work itself, Jaques also proposed a similar scale of complexity of working groups. Figure 2.1 shows a scale inspired by his research. In this model, there are *seven levels of abstraction* reflecting both the degree of *conceptual complexity* and the *time span of the actions* in organisations ('*time horizon*'). There seems to be a direct relationship between conceptual complexity and time span. The first five levels are directly concerned with levels of managerial responsibility in organisations. The last two levels are related to trend, policy and opinion forming.

Levels from Concrete to Abstract		Typical Time Horizon	Description	Approach	Planning
From CONCRETE	1	days	prescribed action	Action follows the rules	doing the task in hand
Direct Command	2	weeks	prescribed output	The rules limit the context of judgement and action	co-ordinating tasks
	3	months	situational response	Extrapolation from a given rule	embryonic, tactical planning of tasks
	4	1 year	systematic service provision	Maintenance of the rule structure	planned tactics (procuring the means)
General or Indirect Command	5	1 to 3 years	comprehensive service provision	Rule-making, thinking outside the rules	embryonic strategy
	6	3 to 10 years	comprehensive field coverage	Policy setting	planned strategy
To ABSTRACT	7	more than 5 to 10 years	environment influence	Trend and society influencing	changing the business environment

Figure 2.1 Levels of Complexity and Time Horizon in Organisations

The scope of a manager's responsibilities is related to the time horizon of the decisions taken at his/her level. These observations are of special interest when considering the maturity of processes, although by necessity they are a simplification of the real world.

In recent years the time horizon tended to shrink, with more emphasis on shorter life-cycles, however the general concepts are still valid.

THE SEI MATURITY MODEL

Research by the Software Engineering Institute (SEI) of Carnegie Mellon University, under the directorship of Watts Humphrey, has made a significant contribution to the understanding of the process of software development, by developing a method for evaluating the strengths and weaknesses of software organisations (Humphrey 1989). This work was motivated by a desire to help organisations engaged in software projects — of all sizes — to make their process better. It identifies a number of levels in which a given project or organisation would find itself — chaotic, repeatable, defined, managed and optimised — and offers a method for improving the quality of its management of the process

The SEI model recognises five levels of process maturity based on the degree of control and formalism displayed by software engineering organisations, as follows:

1) *the initial process:* ad-hoc or 'chaotic', where no orderly progress in process improvement can be made until the process is under statistical control.

2) *the repeatable process:* the organisation has achieved a stable process with a repeatable level of statistical control by initiating rigorous project management of commitments, costs, schedules and changes;

3) *the defined process:* the organisation has defined the process. This helps ensure consistent implementation and provides a basis for a better understanding of the process;

4) *the managed process:* the organisation has initiated comprehensive process measurements and analysis beyond those of cost and schedule performance;

5) *the optimised process:* the organisation now has a foundation for continuous improvement and optimisation of the process.

Watts Humphrey proposes six basic principles which are very relevant to process engineers in general:

- major changes to the (software) process must start at the top;

- everyone must be involved;

- effective changes require knowledge of the current process;

- change is continuous;

- (software) process changes will not be retained without conscious effort and periodic reinforcement;

- (software) process improvement requires investment.

This model is a useful guide for assessing the level of management control over the quality of both the system development process and the outcome —

the software products. Although the process of software development is itself very specific, there are some useful lessons which can inspire a similar research in the maturity of business organisation.

By examining the way an organisation has implemented its activities and is managing them we can also draw some wider conclusions on its status on a 'maturity curve'.

PROCESS MATURITY MODEL

If we take into account the more general environment of business processes and the observations of Elliott Jaques on the way people work, a somewhat different maturity model might be more appropriate. For example, I recommend the adoption of the following seven levels (see Figure 2.2):

- *level 1*: initial state
- *level 2*: repeatable procedures
- *level 3*: documented procedures
- *level 4*: managed processes
- *level 5*: integrated business
- *level 6*: integrated industry
- *level 7*: influenced environment

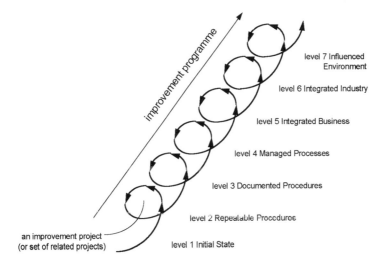

Figure 2.2 *a*BC*d* Business Process Maturity Levels

The seven levels are as follows in more detail:

Level 1 - Initial Stage

Organisations at this level are those where the initiative and 'common sense' of the staff are relied upon to deliver the products or services. Procedures are passed on from mouth to ear or on documents which are usually incomplete and out of date.

Level 2 - Repeatable Procedures

At level 2, procedures exist for the most stable processes as a result of local initiatives, are properly documented and staff adequately trained.

The emphasis for moving to level 2 is on the cultural aspects of the process: the commitment of those involved in built-in quality and process improvement. The objective is to implement and control well-documented procedures and help the organisation members to communicate. The needs in terms of the techniques can be fulfilled with accounting and statistical analysis, requiring relatively unsophisticated modelling techniques such as standard forms and checklists to obtain data and record basic statistics

Level 3 - Documented Procedures

Moving to level 3 offers the opportunity to introduce more analytical methods and the use of diagrams for the description of processes, workflow and document flow modelling and computer-based simulation. The simulation of workflow or document flows can also be used for the actual monitoring of processes.

The basis for a well-managed procedure at level 3 requires more than its documentation and visible management — the interaction between roles and systems also needs to be based on a more analytical understanding of the flow of information or material.

A Total Quality Management (TQM) set of techniques is likely to be introduced at this level. These techniques are now well known (see Gilb 1988 for example) and have been widely applied, although with a variable degree of success. Official terms of reference are available in the form of the International Standards Organisation ISO 9000 and national equivalents such as the French AFNOR, the German DIN and British BS5750 standards. These ratify a minimum level of management control throughout the production or service delivery life-cycle. A large number of medium and large organisations are involved in quality improvement such as TQM projects.

The notion of process becomes clearer at this level but its implementation across functions is not usually challenged. Very often, pen and paper is used to achieve a common understanding, but computer-based assistance can help with the management of the data and with the underlying 'mathematical' parameters (volume, speed, cost). Fairly simple diagrammatic tools and sophisticated simulation tools are used routinely at this level.

Level 4 - Managed Processes

The jump to the next level for an organisation is in recognition that schemes such as ISO 9000 do not adequately address all process issues. Business process re-engineering is used in order to move from level 3 to level 4, which is concerned with inter-function and inter-department processes — the flows of information, documents, materials or goods. Procedures are the backbone of a division or a functional department. But when procedures go beyond the limit of a division or a function, when the work needs to be understood across division or functions, this is when it is necessary to understand the processes.

This level also sees the introduction of the statistical control of variations. This technique was introduced by the statistician Dr W. E. Deming to the Japanese industry after World War II (Deming 1986). It is this technique, and the associated mind set, which made the Japanese industry so competitive on quality in the 1970s and 1980s.

A co-operative effort between functional groups in the organisation is needed to secure an overview of a process. In addition to the cultural complexity there is a conceptual complexity requiring more abstract thinking and modelling using computer-assisted techniques and tools. For instance, process management tools similar to the Role Activity Diagrams (RAD) are one of the most popular in Europe (Ould 1995), whereas IDEF0 is extensively used in the USA for software and system design and for process mapping (Veasey 1993), as discussed in Chapter 12. The use of such tools and techniques in the design or redesign of business processes and for the management of core processes is likely to grow for some time to come.

Level 5 - Integrated Business

The change from level 4 to level 5 is more radical as it involves all the processes supporting the mission of the whole organisation, not only delivering their individual contribution in isolation. The large movement towards greater awareness of such radical business process re-engineering started in the early 1990s (Hammer and Champy 1993) but was in fact pioneered by the work of Dr W. Edward Deming in the 1970s (Deming 1986). We have already mentioned his work in relation to statistical control at level 3. But Deming's philosophy is not merely about statistical control; it embraces a wider concept of the enterprise. It is encapsulated in four core principles:

- *appreciation of the concept of a system*: 'a system is not just composed of divisions, teams, plants, people: these must work together to be a system'.

- *some knowledge of the theory of variation*: although originating from the manufacturing environment, this value has a wider applicability: 'the performance of any component is to be judged in terms *of its contribution to the aim of the system, not* its individual production or profit, nor for any other competitive measure';

- *a theory of knowledge*: 'there is no knowledge without theory, no learning';

- *some knowledge of psychology*: 'ranking individuals on the basis of performance is fundamentally unsound because, with few exceptions, apparent differences in performance mainly result from variations inherent in "the system". Reliance on pay as a motivator destroys pride in work and in individual creativity'.

A growing number of organisations are moving into business redesign programmes at level 5. However, those starting with process re-engineering projects are usually limited in scope to a department or function. The complexity of this redesign calls for the assistance of more analytical and formal techniques supported by computer tools.

Level 6 - Integrated Industry or Partner Integration

Level 6 is where the scope of the process integration goes outside the organisation and brings suppliers into the organisation processes. Japanese manufacturers often operate at level 6, without the benefit of sophisticated computer systems. The strong integrating Japanese culture may be a powerful incentive to operate in that way.

The number of organisations engaged in an integrated system with their suppliers or customers started to grow in the 1990s thanks to the facilitation given by IT through techniques like Electronic Data Interchange (EDI). However, technology is not enough and a proper co-ordinated redesign of the processes and practices of the different partners in the chain is a precondition to successful business integration.

Level 7 - Influenced Environment

Individuals or organisations are operating at level 7 when they are engaged in a fundamental change of the way in which business or public administration is conducted. This is where the revolution takes place in the way information is assessed, the way we work, the way we shop, the way we are entertained, and the way we participate in the public life.

Level 7 is more the province of public or semi-public agencies who manage the future of whole regions or cities, although there are remarkable examples of technical innovators or entrepreneurs like Henry Ford, Thomas Watson Jr or Bill Gates who have changed our way of life.

Mixed Environments

The numbering for business process maturity levels I have adopted is based on Elliott Jaques' 'levels of work abstraction'. Although his results apply to individual attitudes and capabilities, there is a strong correspondence between the concepts describing the maturity of individuals and the process maturity of organisations, at least up to level 6. Level 7 applies more to individuals than organisations.

In a large organisation — larger than a workshop, an office or a shop — each part has to be considered individually and different parts will be at a different level of maturity. This is illustrated by the description given by Edward Guthrie. He said there are roughly three types of warfare: agrarian, industrial and informational, each with its own technology, mind set, processes and style of command (Guthrie 1994). In the US Army, many different units and specialities could be deployed together in a given operation. It is then natural that they will have to work together with processes and technologies belonging to different 'ages' of warfare. In any organisation beyond a few thousand employees, there will be this kind of 'multi-speed' mismatch. In some cases, it might not be desirable to insist that every part undergoes a disruptive regime of change, the preliminary analysis of the priorities for re-engineering will determine which parts are more critical.

Customer Relationship

The notion of value , as discussed in Part III, takes a growing importance from level one to level seven. The first level is basic and reactionary to market needs. A the second level, there are attempts at some understanding of customers' motivations. Level three becomes contractual and customer requirements are stated and documented. At the fourth level, the satisfaction of customers becomes the main focus, beyond compliance with the contract. At the fifth level, the objective is to compete on satisfying the customers better than the competition does. The sixth level emphasises delighting the customers - providing performance beyond that expected or anticipated, by understanding and integrating into their own processes, thus being able to anticipate their needs. The seventh level addresses the restructure of the environment in a way that provides leadership. At each level of the scale, there is a shift in scope from activity to process, from output (measured tasks) to outcome (the effect o the tasks).

PROGRAMME OF CHANGE

The progress of an organisation, or part of an organisation, from one level to another is best managed as a series of projects, each with a definite start date, end date and deliverables. In contrast, the overall programme of change does not always have a specific time span and its goals and achievements are reviewed continuously as experience is accrued. In Figure 2.2, the programme of change is depicted as a series of loops, each being a project or set of related projects.

At each level in the improvement programme, the organisation requires a different set of methods and tools in order to set up an improvement project. These methods and tools are summarised on Figure 2.3 and 2.4.

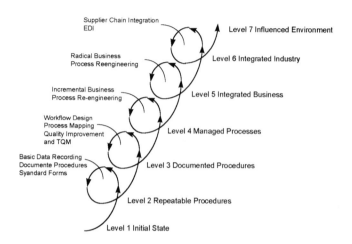

Figure 2.3 Process Improvement and Re-Engineering Techniques

   This model helps us to position the techniques that we have reviewed in the introduction. Traditional process improvement techniques and TQM are relevant when level 2 is the target from level 1. Workflow design and process mapping are specially useful when moving from level 2 to level 3 (and for implementing the processes redesigned at level 4 or 5).

   BPR techniques which seek incremental changes to processes, such as core function analysis, cross-function process flow, value-chain analysis and process simulation, are useful for moving from level 4 to 5. BPR techniques which are more radical, such as value-added modelling and breakthrough management — 'serious creativity' as Edward de Bono said — are required for addressing level 5 (de Bono 1993). The integration of values, the harmonisation of work practices between different organisations and technologies such as (EDI) are relevant for reaching level 6, the industry integration.

Level	Name	Motivation	Design Methods	Tools	Remarks
1	initial		intuitive	pen and paper	
2	repeatable procedures	visibility of control of the process	written procedures	'common sense'	the subject of ISO9000
3	documented procedures	higher efficiency	quality improvement. workflow analysis and design	process mapping, simulation	elimination of waste, financial results
4	managed processes	higher customer service quality	incremental BPR techniques	BPR workbench, facilitation tools	limited scope initiatives, driven by function or department
5	integrated business	higher effectiveness through process integration	radical BPR techniques	automated processes and workflow	driven by senior management
6	integrated industry or partners	faster, cheaper and more effective service to the ultimate customer	vendor-customer integration	automated information transfer (e.g. EDI)	exceptional, driven by monopolies or close interest associations
7	influenced environment	projection of social trends, technological innovations	prospective	simulations, scenarios	the true concept innovation

Figure 2.4 Methods and Tools for Process Maturity

Specific techniques for process design are more relevant to a particular stage of maturity development. It is no use trying a technique which is too sophisticated for the state of development of a particular organisation or area within an organisation. On the other hand, all techniques from a 'less sophisticated' stage are still applicable and are required to implement and improve a redesign process or business.

Software Engineering Processes

Can such a model fit also software development organisations as well as general business organisations? Looking at the whole information systems (IS)department as a candidate for business process redesign, beyond just the software development as addressed by the SEI model, it becomes possible to consider the relationship of the IS department with its suppliers (other vendors) and its customers (the users). The software engineering process can be described in the same way, with a similar maturity profile. However, there is likely to be a growing number of organisations at the higher levels for software engineering compared to business processes, as a consequence of the longer history of using Computer Aided Software Engineering (CASE) methods and tools - which date back to the 1960s. This is illustrated, in a very intuitive fashion, in Figure 2.5.

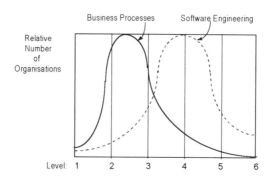

Figure 2.5 Maturity Profiles for Business Processes and Software Engineering Processes

If we compare the history of BPR in the 1990s with the software engineering since the 1980s, we should expect to see a trend in BPR towards more sophisticated methods, more integrated techniques and the use of software-based tools to ensure quality consistency and productivity in redesigning new processes.

There is also a trend towards automating the new processes. Unfortunately, there is the risk of merely automating existing processes. This might achieve some modest gains of productivity but will not result in dramatic changes. Designing effective automated workflow systems requires the redesigning of the processes using a formal and rigorous approach — and then the automation of these processes when appropriate.

CONCLUSION

The maturity of an organisation has been defined in terms of the way it implements and manages its processes using a seven-level process maturity model. This rises from the initial 'level 1' (no visible structure) to the highest 'level 7' (consideration for society and environment). The ambition of a change programme is constrained to follow a step-by-step evolution along the levels: i.e. a particular ambition must take into account the maturity of the organisation and its leaders and their ability to take on new projects and techniques. It is difficult to jump over the steps.

A given organisation will probably have different parts at different levels of maturity. This is especially true if the company is large (typically more than 125 people and more than one department).

Chapter 3

A Framework for Managing Change

INTRODUCTION

We need the intellectual tools to 'engineer' the conceptual concepts in the same way that we engineer the physical world. In this chapter we lay down the rules by which we shall play the design game — a common set of concepts, principles and definitions that have a better chance to be consistent with each other than the use of others, some of which may be better in themselves.

KEY CONCEPTS AND DEFINITIONS

The following subsection introduces a number of key concepts that will be discussed at greater length in later parts of this book. More complete definitions can also be found in Chapter 16.

Process

I define *process* as follows:

> A process is a set of *purposeful* activities, performed by *agents* (people or automatons), supported by *logistical means* (such as IT, communication, manufacture, transportation).

Examples of processes: opening an account, controlling a conflict, designing a product, preparing a meal.

This definition can be complemented by making a distinction between logical process and physical process as follows:

> A logical process is the *abstract description* of a process as a set of related concepts, execution rules, events, preconditions and consequences.

A logical process is not concerned with the physical aspects of specific instances of a process but only with its abstract components.

> A physical process (or business process) is a *particular implementation* of a set of logical processes.

A physical process is constrained by a number of physical or business parameters such as location, size, volume, cost. A business unit is not a business process but a collection of activities identified by a common organisational relationship (location or management).

The *purpose* of a process, or even of an organisation as a whole, is expressed as its outcome — its end-product. In pursuit of that purpose, the process or organisation uses resources, or products from other processes or organisations. The product of a process is a resource for another one. The resulting network forms a complex system that extends beyond the boundary of function, beyond the boundary of a division, even beyond the boundaries of the organisation itself, including suppliers and customers.

Efficiency vs. Effectiveness

The *efficiency* of a process is the ratio Output/Input. Synonyms for efficiency are productivity, waste reduction, best effort. The problem with looking only at the efficiency is that the quality of what is delivered to the customer, the value of the product for that customer, is neglected.

Considering *effectiveness* is about determining first what we want to deliver, then use all the resources to do it effectively. The end point of the process is fixed, it is a matter of improving the process to get there.

It is false to argue that one is better than the other. They both have a role at different times. The following quotation encapsulates this idea perfectly: 'If you want to empty the sea, do it efficiently by using a larger bucket, but if you want to be effective, think of something else to do!' (anon).

Figure 3.1 A Bigger Bucket to Empty the Sea

There are circumstances when it is pointless to try being more efficient. The pursuit of effectiveness is necessary when starting a new venture or a new way of doing things, when we do not know yet the cost and the implication of the new order of things. We do not have enough history for measuring the performance of our operation. After a while, when the new order of things is established, we can turn our attention to improving its efficiency, reducing the cost while maintaining or improving quality.

Surpetition

The notion of *surpetition* (or *Sur/Petition*) was proposed by Edward de Bono as an incentive to companies to be more creative in what they are: 'create your own competition space around your own concepts' thus creating a 'value monopoly' ... 'enter into "*surpetition*" rather than "*competition*" (de Bono 1993). The argument is that every organisation should actively develop its own new concepts which will eventually replace their current offerings. It is a generalisation of the idea of the 'Unique Selling Proposition', differentiating a product from another. When the concept is genuinely new, there is initially no competition, and it will take time before others are able to catch up.

BPR vs. TQM

There is a parallel between the pursuit of effectiveness versus efficiency and surpetition versus competition. In seeking a higher value for customers, a better quality of product or service, an organisation becomes obsessed with effectiveness and ultimately creates its own monopoly. On the other hand, giving priority to efficiency is often the result of increased pressure from competitors or the market. *Surpetition* is about success, *competition* is about survival.

These two considerations are complementary in time: one should succeed the other in a continuous spiral of improvement. BPR and TQM are two sets of techniques which should be used in succession:

> Business Process Reengineering *is best used for seeking effectiveness in 'surpetition' mode*
>
> Total Quality Management *is best used for improving efficiency in 'competition' mode*

Value and Capability

Value is attached to products or resources, to express why a customer is interested in a product and is prepared to pay for it. Value can be described in the form of a specification or a trading description.

In order to encapsulate the importance of value of a resource or a product, the term *capability* is defined in this book as follows:

> A capability is a set of resources or products which are: in a particular *required state*; required by a process or organisation to achieve its objectives; or delivered to a customer, another process or another organisation.

In military terms, a capability is, for example, a division in a particular state of readiness: serviced vehicles, trained personnel, available supplies. The same notion applies to any organisation: a business capability is a set of resources prepared for their purpose, such as documented activities, trained and assigned people, and available *logistical means*.

A process can only deliver a capability for a customer if this represents a value added to the resources for that customer. This capability has to be an integral part of the customer's processes.

This definition of capability is consistent with the discussion in the *Harvard Business Review*, 'competencies and capabilities represent two different but complementary dimensions of an emerging paradigm for corporate strategy. Both concepts emphasise "behavioural" aspects of strategy in contrast to the traditional structural model. But whereas core competencies emphasise technological and production expertise at specific points along the value chain, capabilities are more broadly based, encompassing the entire value chain. In this respect, *capabilities are visible to the customer in a way that core competencies rarely are*' (my emphasis) (Stalk et al 1992).

Capability is a pivotal notion which unifies the different perspectives on an organisation and its relation to its customers and suppliers (see Figure 3.2).

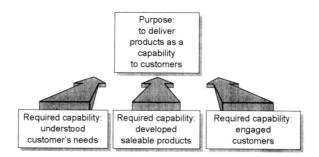

Figure 3.2 The Product of a Process is a Capability for Another Process

This is a very powerful general definition, encompassing examples of capabilities as varied as: a machine in working order; a machine to be repaired; an available squad vehicle; a trained police constable; a working operating theatre; a validated mortgage application; a mobilised tank division; understood customer needs; and a developed saleable product.

- *activity* (an implemented process)

- *people* (players fulfilling roles)

- *logistical   means* (IT, communications, transport, accommodation, storage)

All other resources are subsets of these three classes, e.g. information, data, energy. Money is an attribute of the resources, it is not a resource in itself (except in very rare cases), although in practice we can transform money into the other resources. From a design point of view, this obscures the proper definition of the resources needed by a process.

In Part III, we shall introduce techniques for analysing capabilities and values. Figure 3.3 shows the notation that we would use with these techniques to show the value-added relationship of Figure 3.2.

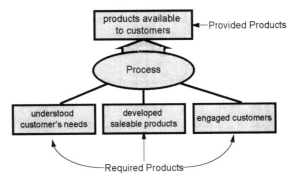

Figure 3.3 Value-Added Diagram

Core Competency

A core competency for an organisation is the combination of individual technologies and production skills that underlay a company's different product lines (Stalk et al 1992). Core competencies are not the same as core capabilities as I have just defined them.

THE KEY BUSINESS PERSPECTIVES

Human and Social Dimensions

Models are instruments for reducing the complexity of organisations under study. They allow us to abstract from the real world, highlighting the things and the relationships which are of interest and ignoring those which are too specific.

The simplest model of an organisation is the traditional organisation chart showing the reporting structure (see Figure 3.4). This is a neat document to start with but it gets more and more obscure as the organisation grows in size and sophistication, when hierarchical line reporting and more horizontal product or market relationships interfere with each other. It completely breaks down in a devolved or federalist structure.

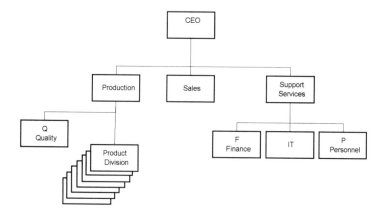

Figure 3.4 A Typical Organisation Chart

With the advent of the mighty computer, information scientists imposed their culture and modelled the enterprise as a giant labyrinth of pipes conveying data to all parts of the organisation. Processes are merely there to transform information, the models are not models of reality but of the way information about reality is processed by people and machines. Computer scientists have been traditionally uncomfortable with things which cannot be reduced to data. The cartoon shown in Figure 3.5, from an anonymous artist (please come forward for recognition), expresses the consequences in a nutshell.

"Your pointing at it won't help -
the computer record shows none in stock!"

Figure 3.5 The Only Real Thing is the Computer
(With apologies to the now untraceable author)

In parallel with the IT revolution, systems theory has made a valuable contribution to business management by offering a view in which the various functions of the enterprise could be reunited and reconciled with its environment. Systems theory was formalised by Ludwig von Bertalanffy in the early 1960s (von Bertalanffy 1966). The seminal independent works of Dr W.E. Deming and Beer have extended its application further to the field of management of manufacturing and public services respectively (Deming 1986 and Beer 1966).

From this perspective, an organisation is viewed as a complex system but responding to simple mechanisms. Every part makes a contribution to the whole and cannot be justified or explained without it. This is recognised in systems theory through notions like input, output, feedback loop, transformation, influences and dependencies.

There is also a cultural dimension to complicate matters and prevents the best designed theoretical constructions working as planned. This demands the involvement of anthropologists, social scientists and organisational behaviour specialists to help sort out what does not fit into information and systems theories. By showing the similarity between the life of a purposeful organisation and that of any society of human beings, they are helping us to reconsider people from a different viewpoint than the mere 'management' of people.

Of course, each of these views is valid because they show what we see if we stand at different points of the conceptual domain. The danger is to assume that only one is necessary, the difficulty is to reconcile them with a harmonious understanding which enables us to design better organisations.

The scope of this book focuses on the techniques of process design. This deals mainly with the non-cultural aspects of processes because the cultural dimension is not yet so easy to formalise.

THE FOUR MAIN VIEWS OF AN ORGANISATION

We need to reduce the complexity of actual organisations by finding out if there are perspectives which are more or less independent from each other. This can be done by considering four views:

1) the organisational;

2) the logical;

3) the physical; and

4) the informational.

The 'Vertical' Organisational View

The organisational chart, often showing a hierarchical, management structure, documents the organisational view that, by convention, I shall call 'the *vertical view*'. There is no particular reason why I call it the 'vertical view' possibly because the traditional chart illustrates a hierarchical management structure with a top and a bottom (see Figure 3.6).

The organisational chart does not explain how the organisation works but it is an instrument for showing how we cope with a large number of people and a diversity of locations: 'headquarters, regional offices and local branches', or 'industrial vehicles and domestic cars', or 'UK, Europe, Far East and the Rest of the World'. The hierarchical structure is the result of a desire to reduce the number of people reporting to a manager or director, down to a comfortable number.

The 'Vertical Dimension'

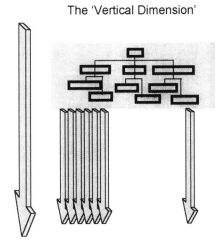

Used to understand and document
locations and reporting organisation

Figure 3.6 The 'Vertical' Organisational View

The organisational view is concerned essentially with documenting the *location and grouping of people* and the *business constraints* — where, how often, how fast operations need to be performed (see Figure 3.6). For example, a banking business may have 256 branches and one HQ, each of them could be engaged in a number of transactions. One of these transactions might be *'opening an account'*, taking place all the time at different places in different forms: current account, savings account or loan.

The real world is messy and this is reflected in most real organisation charts. In summary:

> The *vertical, organisational view* describes an organisation in terms of its business units, the reporting organisation, the location and grouping of people and the business constraints.

The 'Horizontal' Logical View

If we consider again the transaction *'opening an account'*, we may feel intuitively that there must be a way to describe a type of transaction 'opening account' that is generic, independent of a particular location, a particular branch or a particular customer. We should be able to document the concepts in this type of transaction, the states of these concepts, the roles and generic resources required to complete it and its measurements - its Performance Indicators (PI). The collection of these entities constitutes the abstract, logical, generic model of the transactions, and more generally the processes.

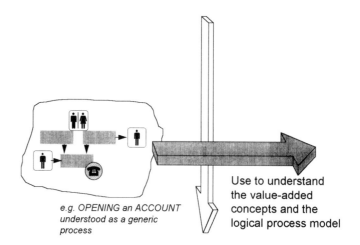

Figure 3.7 The 'Horizontal' Logical Process Model

The 'horizontal' dimension is sometimes used in organisation charts to document the reuseable skills or resources (e.g. IT, Human Resources, Plant Maintenance, Purchasing, etc.). I shall refer to this dimension as the logical dimension, showing the reuseable logical (abstract) business components found across the organisation.

These logical components are defined with the help of the value analysis techniques (see Part III). They include approaches and policies, logical processes, roles, system definitions, entity types, event types, and reuseable implementation types. These are the abstract, generic components, not the implemented, physical ones.

The resulting model is the architecture of the processes, a non-redundant description of the generic processes: in which any given logical process will be found at only one place in the model. This is known as a *normalised* model, to use a data modelling term. When we want to understand the usage and states of an entity, we will find it in the context where it is relevant. For example, the generic process *'opening an account'* will be found at only one place in the model.

Dr W.E. Deming states in his *Theory of Knowledge* that: 'experience, in the absence of theory, teaches *nothing*. Without theory, we have no questions, we learn nothing, all people can do is copy, and then wonder what's the matter' (Deming 1991). The result of value analysis is a form of theory, a set of concepts and a language to talk about the process under study. With experience we can refine the logical model — the theory — to explain what is going on in the physical world.

Although the real world is messy, we can afford to be neat in its abstract model. 'A city is not a tree' said the great architect Christopher Alexander, and this applies also to organisations. But even a town can be modelled with a neat network of straight lines, like the London Underground map. To summarise:

> The *'horizontal'* logical abstract view of an organisation is used to model the set of concepts and the language to talk about the processes under study. It contains the process architecture, a normalised model of the processes, business entities and events that can be reused across the organisation.

The 'Diagonal' Physical View

The combination of the vertical and the horizontal dimensions results in the 'diagonal' dimension, the 'physical view', where we want to localise instances of the logical processes, where we design implementable processes, where we need to devise physical solutions — the activities performed in business units — and to specify the resource requirements. For completing this task we have available the business constraints - organisation, size, volume, frequency, speed, urgency, priority, budgets - and the logical understanding of the generic reuseable components of the business (see Figure 3.8).

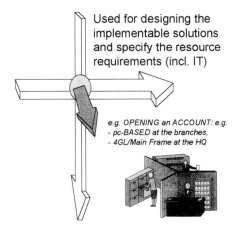

Figure 3.8 The 'Diagonal' Physical View

For example, in implementing the process *'opening an account'* in a specific business unit such as a small branch, we may devise a solution in the shape of a procedure to be followed by staff who are engaged in other activities and using a small computer system with a package written for that system. At HQ, on the other hand, we may have a team of people dedicated to this activity, using a mainframe computer with a dedicated mainframe application. The activities in branches and HQ will look different because their business environment is different. Without the benefit of the logical model, it would be difficult to integrate them. It is also difficult to reuse the solution devised for one environment into another one. In brief:

> The *'diagonal'* physical view of an organisation is used to specify and implement instances of logical processes in the context of business units.

The Informational View

For the convenience of information system designers, an informational view of organisations is sometimes advocated. In fact this is useful for IT designers but not for process designers. Information is not a separate resource to be managed independently from the organisation. Information is the organisation. It is the expression of the concepts which 'makes it tick'. Without information, a business is a wasted land of things and people. To manage it separately is to create big problems. People will then, over time, by-pass the implemented systems in order to respond more appropriately to concepts that they perceive are more up to date. This leads to the development of 'informal' or clandestine systems and procedures. So we shall not treat information as a separate view but as an integral part of the organisational, logical and physical views.

Summary of the Modelling Views

In summary, we must consider three dimensions of an organisation corresponding to the organisational, the logical and the physical views. We must, however, keep in mind that these dimensions correspond to the same reality. For convenience, we will use different notations but will ensure that a common terminology is used where they apply to the same things.

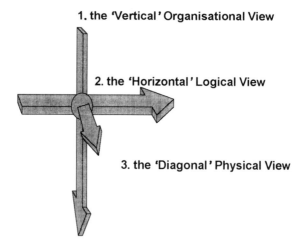

Figure 3.9 The Three Views on a Business

In designing the processes, with the participation of the people affected by them, we will need to be sensitive to the prevailing way of working of the organisation. This cultural perspective is especially important in the change from the current situation to the new one.

> The organisational, logical and physical views of an organisation are necessary and sufficient to design business processes. But the cultural implications must also be taken into account for a successful implementation.

CONCLUSIONS

Business Process Design is best used in pursuit of increased effectiveness through radical change projects. Efficiency is best addressed in between periods of radical changes with other techniques such as TQM. There are three viewpoints from which we can look at an organisation for process design: organisational, logical and physical. This provides a framework for deploying the most appropriate analysis and design techniques. The method - the route map - for undertaking process design projects will be reviewed in the next chapter.

Chapter 4

Planning Change Programmes

INTRODUCTION

In the introduction, we saw how every organisation, if left to its own fate, goes through a predictable life of birth, growth and decline. A renewal programme must be initiated before it is to late so that we can undertake a radical step change when it becomes clear that nothing else will sustain the past successes.

In the previous chapter we have set the framework and the concepts for process design; in this chapter we shall see how we can support sustainable programmes of change within that framework.

ORGANISATION FOR CHANGE

The scope of a change project can vary from a single task to the organisation as a whole, but only the most senior management can initiate changes that affect the whole enterprise or the more fundamental core processes. If the scope of change exceeds a single project, it is necessary to set up a programme of change — a framework for several co-ordinated projects — and a specific 'organisation for change' with specific senior management responsibility.

In this programme, a useful guide is provided by the Socratic saying: 'When you always do what you have always done, you always get what you always got'. Experience has shown that it is practically impossible to mix change with daily operation. The pressure of everyday work will always have priority over less urgent tasks. All the constraints and performance measurements are geared up to prevent changes. It is then best to nurture 'off-line' change projects in order to design and test the proposed new processes. Performing the switchover from the existing processes could then be made at an appropriate time.

Each organisation will have its own ideas on how to set up such a change programme. In some cases, a special department reporting to senior management could co-ordinate the programme. It would acquire the expertise to facilitate the carrying out of projects using the contributions of people with solid business experience, drawn from the affected business units at managerial and operational levels.

In other cases, a small team close to the senior executives could supervise and monitor highly motivated 'seed facilitators' who are briefed and trained for spreading the vision and the initiative enthusiastically throughout the business.

In all cases, the help of external consultants could speed up the learning curve and would bring in fresh and unbiased ideas and guidance. But no organisation can be 're-engineered' by external consultants. The thinking and redesign should be conducted by the people with the real experience of the business.

When it is possible to identify projects, either as part of the redesign of the business as a whole, or as an isolated or limited initiative, it is easier to formalise the project phases. In the following sections, we shall see a typical method which can be followed for such a project.

PROCESS DESIGN METHODS

A method is a series of steps to follow in order to achieve the desired result. For each step, there are expected results and identified deliverables — for example, a mission statement, a logical model, a set of activity flow diagrams, specifications for roles and competencies. The techniques to use for producing these results can vary and depend on the preference of the design team and their familiarity with particular approaches (see Figure 4.1). In this book, I propose the default set of techniques contained within the *a*BC*d* method but there are often other acceptable alternatives.

method:	deliverables:	techniques:	tools:

step 1			
⇨1.1 ----	d1, d2	a, b	tool 1
⇨1.2 ----	d3	c	tool 2

for *example*:

step 4 Define Logical Process			
⇨4.1 priority area	scope of model	facilitated workshop	Flip Chart and Word processor
⇨4.2 define VAD	value-added model	value analysis	aBCd workbench
⇨4.3 define concepts	concept model	value analysis	aBCd workbench
⇨4.4 define bus. events	event model	value analysis	aBCd workbench
⇨4.5 quality review	walk through session	Fegan review	Flip Chart and Word processor

Figure 4.1 The Relationship between Method, Deliverables, Techniques and Tools

Each situation is unique, each organisation and each project is different and it is inappropriate to force-fit an off-the-shelf method — however powerful this solution might be. Each project will have its own method, its own set of steps. The leader of the redesign programme must adapt the approach to each situation and keep control of the approach which is suitable to each project.

ROAD MAPS FOR PROCESS IMPROVEMENT AND REDESIGN

Using general problem-solving principles (Fisher and Ury 1991), the typical steps of a process design project would include the four broad phases shown in Figure 4.2:

- *the What Phase*: clarifies the direction, and the current situation, problems and issues, setting up the organisation for change;

- *the With Phase*: formalises the process architecture, the value contents of the end-product or service, and designs the capabilities and generic implementable processes required to deliver your mission;

- *the How Phase*: decides the way to actually implement the processes and detailed activities within the business constraints: qualifying and quantifying the required capabilities - formally and in practical implementable terms, negotiating the procurement of the resources required;

- *the When Phase*: implements an evolution through projects.

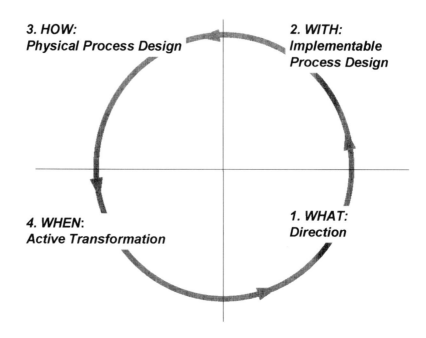

Figure 4.2 The *a*BC*d* Process of Process Improvement

Sustaining Improvement

By repeating the What Phase activities of measuring results and formulating further projects, it becomes possible to maintain a cycle of continuous process improvement, whose general route map is shown in Figure 4.3. This shows also the deliverables required in each phase:

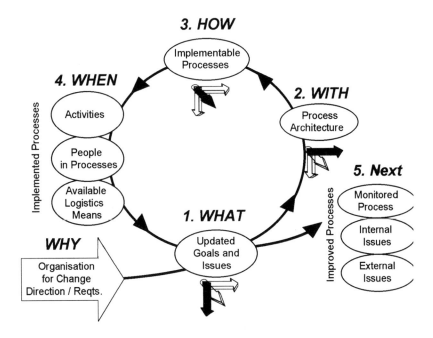

Figure 4.3 Large Scale *a*BC*d* Route Map for Process Improvement

Figure 4.3 shows the cycle in graphical form.

The general route map for process improvement is captured in the diagram shown on Figure 4.3 where we can see the deliverables of each phase:

1) *Updated Goals and Current Issues*: confirm overall direction, clarify the end-products required to fulfil that mission (the goals and objectives), understand the current situation and issues;

2) *Process Architecture*: design the generic processes required to meet the goals;

3) *Implementable Processes*: translation of the process architecture into activities which can be implemented in the actual organisation, including the management processes;

4) *Implemented Physical Processes*: revised or new processes actually implemented - activities, people in processes and *logistical* means - (usually sub-contracted to specialist providers), replacing the existing processes by the redesigned ones;

5) *Improved Processes*: measure and monitor how well the redesigned processes contribute to the goals, encourage and manage the generation of issues reports, assess achievements — similar to phase 1 but in preparation for further improvements.

Deming Cycle

Dr W.E. Deming proposed a method for process improvement which is very similar in its broad lines to the method that we are following. The Deming cycle can be described with the FOCUS-PDCA acronym (Walton 1990):

The FOCUS comes in setting up the change programme:

- *Find* a process
- *Organise* the teams
- *Clarify* the current knowledge
- *Understand* the causes of process variations
- *Select* the process

PDCA was defined by Deming for carrying out a number of projects through a 'Plan, Do, Check, Act' cycle. This can be adapted to the process improvement cycle in Figure 4.2 as follows:

- *Check* results: understand the problems
- *Act*: analyse the problem, decide actions
- *Plan* actions and solutions
- *Do* improvements

Each activity now corresponds broadly to the What, With, How, When considerations that have been adopted with *a*BC*d* and which will be developed below.

	Deming Stage	Process Design Stage
1	CHECK	WHAT
2	ACT	WITH
3	PLAN	HOW
4	DO	WHEN

Figure 4.4 The Deming Cycle and Process Design Stages

The original ideas of Deming were much more radical than the limited scope of quality improvement which is commonly adopted by his followers. Quality improvement indeed has its place and is a method which has been proved valuable in improving the efficiency of processes, sometimes in spectacular ways (Deming 1991). However, it is not usually the ambition or the terms of references of the quality improvement team to challenge the reason for or the design of the process under study.

Problem Solving Cycle

It should not be a surprise to find that the steps for solving problems have also been expressed as a similar four-phase process (Fisher and Ury 1991):

	IN THEORY	IN THE REAL WORD
WHAT IS WRONG	*Step 2. Analysis (WITH)* Diagnose the problem: sort symptoms into categories. Suggest causes. Observe what is lacking. Note barriers to resolving the problem.	*Step 1. Problem (WHAT)* What is wrong? What are the current symptoms? Why do the disliked facts contrast with the real situation?
WHAT MIGHT BE DONE	*Step 3. Approaches (HOW)* What are possible strategies or prescriptions. What are some theoretical cures? Generate broad ideas of what might be done.	*Step 4. Action Ideas (WHEN)* What might be done? What specific steps might be taken to deal with the problem?

Figure 4.5 Four Generic Stages in Solving Problems

Fisher positions the four phases of problem solving in a two-by-two space: reality/theory and problem/solution arriving at a similar construction as Checkland with the Soft System Methodology. This is an additional good justification for our four-phase process improvement cycle.

Soft Systems Methodology

Professor Peter Checkland from Lancaster University was one of the earlier advocates of the application of systems theory to 'messy' real life management problems. Checkland's 'Soft Systems Methodology' (SSM)) rests on the theory of systems and reconciliates what is happening in the 'real world' with the abstract domain of the concepts (Checkland and Scholes 1990). There is a similarity between our approach and the method proposed by Checkland. This is clear from Figure 4.6 where the SSM method is illustrated.

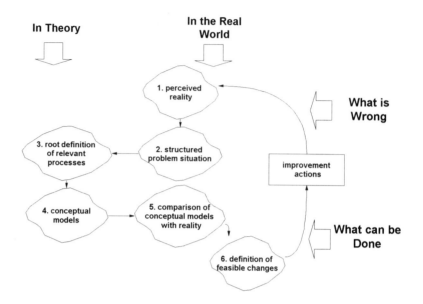

Figure 4.6 Soft Systems Methodology Process

The approaches discussed in this book as part of *a*BC*d* are complementary to the work of Deming and Checkland. The *a*BC*d* techniques and underpinning coherent theory of processes, however, could make improvement projects faster and deliver results more resilient to changes in the environment.

THE KEY ELEMENTS OF PROCESS DESIGN: ACTIVITY, PEOPLE AND LOGISTICAL MEANS

Any resource used by an organisation can be classified as one of three:

- activities;

- people;

- logistical means.

Activities include the process documentation in the form of procedures, know-how, rules, ethics, policies. The people aspect includes the role descriptions, the training, the competency framework. *Logistical* means encompass IT systems, workflow systems, communication, transports, manufacturing and storage plants.

Money is a means of acquiring any of the other resources. Money is a kind of common measurement of the effort in acquiring them. Except in very specific cases, where it is itself the object of the processing, money should not be a resource worth modelling in process design.

LEARNING BY DOING

When a captain steers a ship through difficult waters, the route can be plotted on a map because the starting point and the end point are known. In contrast the steering of an organisation through difficult times does not have a charted end point. This situation is more like the travels of the early explorers into uncharted waters. It was the duty of the captain - and the crew - to learn as they went along — learning by doing. The route map proposed in the previous sections is only a generic map which must be detailed and adapted with the active contribution of all the crew.

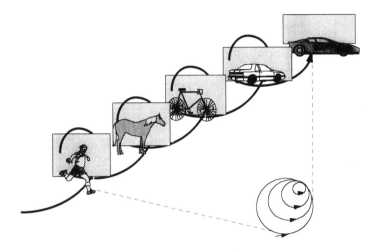

Figure 4.7 Change Programme as a Series of Improvement Projects

It is rare to be able to design a new process or organisation from scratch in the mythical 'green field'. And performing radical changes on live organisations is always rather traumatic. The disruption can be reduced if the radical change can be implemented as a series of smaller leaps as illustrated on Figure 4.7. Each leap is performed as controlled projects, with a beginning, an end and measurable deliverables. This provides an opportunity for learning by doing. It is an approach followed by a number of organisations, such as the National & Provincial Building Society, a British financial institution engaged in a radical programme of changes. Once the initial radical changes in the management structure and style, with the necessary cultural changes, were in place, each of the operational processes was tackled as controlled projects (O'Brien and Wainwright 1993).

Learning from experience must be institutionalised so that problems, failures and other issues really become seen as opportunities for improving the process and the way people and resources are managed. The understanding of process design has an interesting side-effect in promoting a culture of 'no-blame', design has an interesting side-effect in promoting a culture of 'no-blame', where people should be encouraged to report problems so that the process can be improved rather than be under the threat of personal penalties. Of course we should not be naive enough to believe that the problem always comes from the process, but it is probably true in many cases. Margaret Edge, a manager of process redesign in a large service organisation, is reported to say that an essential belief in process design is that 'people can do things. It is essential to create a no blame culture which can only be achieved by keeping communication channels open' (Milne 1995).

A consequence of this approach is to institutionalise change as a normal part of the life of the organisation. It becomes clear to the participants that change is not a single leap but is an on-going reality. However, this must be carefully managed because too much change, too often, does not give enough opportunity for quality and efficiency improvement in between major changes. Too frequent changes also affect badly the morale and effectiveness of the individuals suffering them and often leads to complete demotivation and failure.

ISSUES MANAGEMENT

Issues is the term that we use for describing the problems, the suggestions, the ideas that are generated during the design and the operational life of processes. In a 'no-blame' culture, every member of the organisation has the duty to identify and document what they identify as issues, with the confidence that in most cases, the issues are caused by process 'design faults' rather than by the fault of individuals. The nature of the issues could be relevant to implementation, design or direction.

SUSTAINED IMPROVEMENTS

In system theory, a stable system is described as having a feedback loop that is used to compare the actual outcome of a system to the desired one and to take action to reduce the difference (see Figure 4.8). This is exactly what we are trying to put in place when we have the elements for a sustainable system: a specification of the desired 'signal' (direction and objectives), an improvement engine (the process design and improvement projects), an output (the effect on the organisation), a measurement of the performance and identified issues (the clues of low performance) and an 'error signal' - the comparison between the achievements and the desired performance.

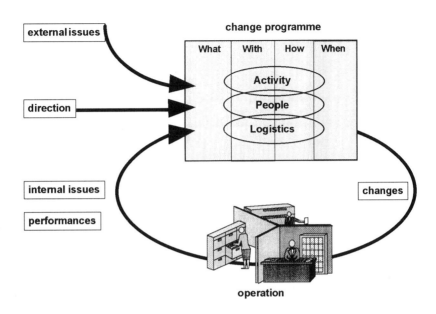

Figure 4.8 Process Improvement as a Sustainable System

PRIORITY OF IMPROVEMENTS

In general, it is not realistic nor desirable to change all the processes in an organisation. The ideal situation, from a process designer's point of view, is when everything is possible, when there is no need to keep the current organisation running or when we can stop, re-engineer the processes and start again. Unfortunately, such a 'green field' site is almost never seen in reality. It seems impossible to design even brand new organisations from scratch. This is probably due to human nature: the members of the new management team have been selected for their experience elsewhere and thus bring their own way of doing things, their own good or bad habits. There is also the pressure to show early tangible results and experience shows that 'practicality' gets in the way of 'rationality'. It is only after the teams have started to operate as new social entities, and have met their first difficulties, that they would consider engineering or re-engineering their processes. The aBCd maturity model proposed in Chapter 2 could help to understand where an organisation stands in its first months or years of existence.

So in most cases, there is a need to identify and prioritise the change initiatives and to derive improvement projects to implement them. A short audit of the current situation will provide the information supporting this planning. In assigning a priority to the change projects, we want to consider the core capabilities needed to meet the goals of the organisation and the performance indicators of the current capabilities.

Key Performance Indicators

In Chapter 6, dedicated to the management architecture, I shall give a more precise meaning to what we mean by goals, core — or critical — processes, and critical success factors. We shall see that the mission of the organisation should be refined in terms of goals directed at its main stakeholders, and in particular its customers, employees, suppliers and shareholders. The objectives are quantified goals. The core processes are those delivering these goals. The *Key Performance Indicators (KPI)*, sometimes called Critical Success Factors (CSF), are the measurements of achievement of the objectives, used to monitor the performance of the core processes.

In order to identify the opportunity for improving existing processes or functions, we shall assess two quantities: the importance of their contribution to the objectives of the organisation (their *strategic* importance) and the relative value of their KPIs (their *performance*). We do not need to be very precise and we should not spend too much time seeking a higher accuracy of the measurements. In fact, experienced managers are often able to provide a fairly representative set of measurements from their own intuition.

Examples of KPI could include: 'reduced warranty failure of product in the field'; 'improved response to customers'; 'improved quality of customer communication'. Processes or functions will be assigned a degree of criticality in meeting the organisation objectives. A relative scale such as Low, Medium and High, or a numerical scale from 0 to 10 or 0 to 100 can be used to express the strategic importance. Core processes with a high score could be, for example, 'understanding customer needs'; 'acquiring new customers'; 'engaging customers'; 'developing staff competency'; 'monitoring the impact of regulation'; 'developing new products'. In Part III, dedicated to value analysis, we shall review techniques for understanding and defining these core processes more systematically.

Evaluating the Relative Importance of Processes

The result of an analysis as outlined above will be a diagram such as Figure 4.9. This shows a graph plotting the processes under consideration, with their *strategic importance* (the expected relevance to the KPIs) on the horizontal axis and the current performance (actual contribution to direction and goals) on the vertical axis, increasing from top to bottom. The candidate processes for improvement are found in the top right-hand corner of the plot. They can be ranked in decreasing order of need. As a first cut, the analysts can volunteer their intuitive appreciation of the scores. When time and resource permit, they can quantify these scores more accurately. People usually undervalue their own intuition, although the intuitive scores are usually broadly confirmed in practice.

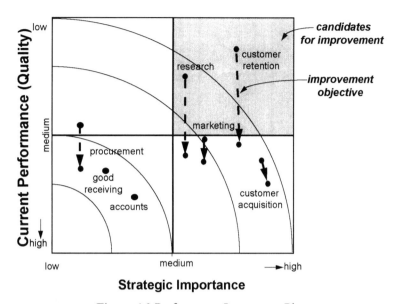

Figure 4.9 Performance-Importance Plot

We can also show on the diagram the position that each process needs to have according to the strategic or tactical plan and the shift that must be achieved by the improvement projects. Decision analysis can be used to understand the consequences of the available options and to apportion the improvement budget between the various candidate projects. We shall review these techniques in Chapter 13.

CONCLUSION

Having set the scene for improvement programmes in general, we need to come down to the reality of projects. In Part II, we shall review a generic template from which these projects can be drawn up.

Part II
Generic Management and Planning Activities

Chapter 5

Process Improvement Projects

INTRODUCTION

A programme of change consists of a number of process improvement projects undertaken in series or in parallel. In this chapter we shall review a generic route map for undertaking these projects, documented as a set of phases. This offers a 'menu' from which the project manager and the programme steering team directing the changes can tailor projects to be appropriate to each situation.

IMPROVEMENT PROJECTS

Off-Line or On-Line?

An improvement project requires strict management discipline in which defined activities have expected outputs — the process changes, expressed as new capabilities — and a specified start date, end date, and agreed budget. Such projects should be undertaken 'off-line', out of the normal day-to-day running of the operation. This is because experience shows that the pressure to perform daily activities always takes precedence over additional change tasks (Pellegrinelli and Bowman 1994). When the study of new solutions has produced practical proposals which can be planned and contracted to development teams, the responsibility for phasing them into the organisation returns to the people involved in the operation. This study should be quite short — about two to six weeks.

We can use the Process Maturity Model, introduced in the previous chapter, to justify each improvement project. Such a project is a measure directed at moving the organisation from one level of maturity to the next one in a specific aspect. For example, a project could be concerned with implementing a competency system in an organisation which already operates a traditional, controlled appraisal system. Another example could be an improvement of the customer engagement process from fragmented department-based customer services.

Project Management

Project management techniques are widely used in many industries, from civil engineering to software development. For example the PRINCE methodology has been adopted for projects in Europe (NCC 1990 and Bradley 1993). PRINCE is especially appealing because its project management principles and guidelines are universal and relevant to any type of projects, including quality improvement, process re-engineering, Human Resources or IT development. The clearly defined management structure of a project run under PRINCE ensures that the interests of the main stakeholders in a project are properly represented in terms of:

- the funding of the project (*the business perspective*);
- the delivered capabilities (*the user's perspective*);
- the project activities (*the developer's perspective*).

Figure 5.1 shows a simple organisation for a PRINCE-run project.

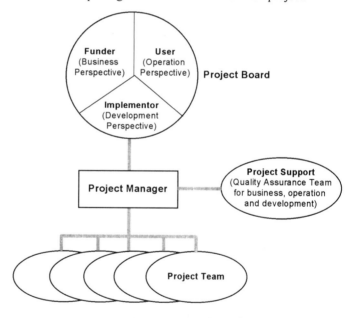

Figure 5.1 Organisation of a Project Run with PRINCE

These interests are often conflicting and the issues are resolved by a *Project Board* comprising executives representing each perspective. A number of individuals or interest groups can represent these diverse interests but with a clearly defined separation of concerns. The board must have the necessary authority for directing the project and in particular for agreeing the initial and changed budget, resources, requirements and approaches.

The role of *Project Manager* in PRINCE is not usually divided and should be assumed by one individual. The project manager receives the directives from the Project Board and leads the project teams, each responsible for a phase or a specialist development. Reporting the results and issues to the Board is part of that role.

PROJECT TEMPLATES

Each project is concerned with changing one aspect of the process maturity level. A project template can be expressed as a *work breakdown* showing the tasks, deliverables and techniques which are applicable to each task, together with the tools supporting the techniques. In the work breakdown, we should recognise the now familar considerations: WHAT, WITH, HOW and WHEN discussed in Chapter 4. The generic *a*BC*d* work breakdown could be as follows:

	Step	**Consideration**
1.	Initiate the Project	Project Management
2.	Identify Current Maturity Level	WHAT
3.	Identify Maturity Requirements	WHAT
4.	Define Logical Processes	WITH
5.	Define Implementable Processes	WITH
6.	Define Implementation Solutions	HOW
7.	Define Evolution Plan	WHEN
8.	Present Project Results	Project Management

Figure 5.2 The *a*BC*d* Generic Project Steps

The detail of these steps is as follows.

Main Step 1: Initiate the Project

The first step is to set up the organisation of the project, the reporting structure and the composition of the team(s) and the schedule.

No	Task Description	Deliverable	Technique	Tool
1.1	Review Related Studies	Study Notes	Field Investigation, Workshops	Word Processor
1.2	Produce Project Brief	Project Brief	Project Management Technique	Word Processor
1.3	Produce Quality Plan	Quality Plan	Management Technique	Word Processor
1.4	Formalise Project Control	Quality Plan	Management Technique	Word Processor
1.5	Define Management Reporting	Quality Plan	Management Technique	Word Processor
1.6	Produce Schedule	Project Schedule	Project Planning	Project Management Software
1.7	Conduct Team Training	Workshop Reviews	Tutorial or Computer-Based Training	Word Processor
1.8	Review Project Initiation	Quality Review	Walk Through	Word Processor

It is always good practice to plan a quality review of the results as the last task of a phase or step. This could be part of a formal presentation of the results to the project board by the project manager, supported by their respective teams.

Main Step 2: Identify Current Maturity Level

In this step we confirm the scope of the project in relation to the maturity model. This step, with the following step 3, addresses the 'WHAT?' question.

No	Task Description	Deliverable	Technique	Tool
2.1	Assess Processes	Assessment Report	Enquiries and Facilitation	Facilitated Workshops, Analysis Tool
2.2	Assess Current Direction Contribution	Assessment Report	Enquiries and Facilitation	Facilitated Workshops
2.3	Assess Measurements and Outstanding Issues	Assessment Report	Enquiries and Facilitation	Facilitated Workshops
2.4	Assess Improve-ment and Inno-vation Potential	Assessment Report	Enquiries and Facilitation	Facilitated Workshops
2.5	Identify Maturity Level	Maturity Report		Word Processor
2.6	Review Current Assessment	Quality Review	Walk Through Inspection	Word Processor

Main Step 3: Identify Maturity Requirements

This step is concerned with reviewing the current situation, the outstanding issues and with confirming the organisation direction requirements.

Task	Task Description	Deliverable	Technique	Tool
3.1	Identify and Analyse the Outstanding Issues	Analysed and Prioritised Issues	Cause-Effect Analysis	Cause-Effect Analysis Tool
3.2	Map the current process if applicable	Mapped process	Process Mapping	Mapping Tool*, Design Tool** or Drawing Tool
3.3	Identify required Maturity Level	Maturity Requirements	Maturity Model	Questionnaire, Check List
3.4	Prioritise Improvement Requirements	Prioritised Requirements	Performance-Importance Matrix	Graphic Modeller, Presentation
3.5	Identify Process Mgt Requirements	Management Architecture	Management Model	Text and Graphical Modelling Tool
3.6	Identify Measurement Requirements	Measurement Requirements	Field Investigation	Text Processor or Modelling Tool
3.7	Identify Innovation Opportunities	Innovation Opportunities	Technology Investigations	Publication Scans, Text Processor
3.8	Review Maturity Requirements	Quality Review	Walk Through Inspection	Word Processor

* A mapping tool is a drawing tool specialised to the representation of processes in graphical form.
** A design tool is a drawing tool with consistency checks and levelling (decomposition) capabilities, specialised to the design of processes.

Main Step 4: Define Logical Processes

This contributes to construct the logical model of the organisation, in the specific area of the project. This step addresses the 'WITH?' question.

No	Task Description	Deliverable	Technique	Tool
4.1	Confirm Priority of Study Area	Scope of Model	Facilitated Workshop	Word Processor
4.2	Define Value-Added Products	Value-Added Model	Value Analysis	Design Tool or Drawing Tool
4.3	Define Concept and Event Model	Concept Model	Value Analysis	Design Tool or Drawing Tool
4.4	Define Critical Concepts and Events	Event Model	Value Analysis	Design Tool or Drawing Tool
4.5	Review Logical Process Model	Quality Review	Walk Through Inspection	Word Processor

Main Step 5: Define Implementable Processes

This step also addresses the 'WITH?' question by defining the implementable activities (still generic).

No	Task Description	Deliverable	Technique	Tool
5.1	Produce Activity Model	Activity Model	Process Mapping	Design Tool or Drawing Tool
5.2	Design Team Structures	Roles/Responsibility	Team Architecture	Design Tool or Drawing Tool
5.3	Define Quality Measures	Capability Model	Value Analysis	Design Tool or Spread Sheet
5.4	Review and Validate Model	Quality Review	Walk Through Inspection	Word Processor and Diagrams

Main Step 6: Define Implementation Solutions

In this step we take into account the business constraints, the current and required competencies, and the physical context for which we shall propose actual solutions. This should answer the 'HOW?' question.

No	Task Description	Deliverable	Technique	Tool
6.1	Define Organisation (Management)	Management Framework	Process Management Model	Design Tool or Word Processor
6.2	Define Physical Processes	Physical Activities	Process Mapping	Design Tool and Simulation
6.3	Define Human Resources Means (Roles)	Roles and Competencies	Competency Model, Specification Techniques	Design Tool
6.4	Define *Logistical* Support Means	*Logistical* Means Solutions	Process Mapping, Specification Techniques	Word Processor
6.5	Define Technology	Technology Solutions	Technology Watch, Specification Techniques	Word Processor
6.6	Review and Integrated Design	Quality Review	Walk Through Inspection	Word Processor

Main Step 7: Define Evolution Plan

In this step we define the development plan for the specialised developments which will be undertaken by, for example, Human Resources or IT contractors. This is the answer to 'WHEN?'.

No	Task	Deliverable	Technique	Tool
7.1	Define Projects	Project Briefs	Specification Methods	Word Processor Project Management
7.2	Define Dependencies	PERT Chart	Decision Analysis, Physical Process Design	Decision Analysis Tool and Project Management Software Process Design Tool
7.3	Specify Resources	PERT Chart	Decision Analysis, Budgeting	Decision Analysis Tool and Project Management Software
7.4	Define Schedule	Gantt Chart	Project Planning	Project Management Software
7.5	Review Evolution Plan	Quality Review	Walk Through Inspection	Word Processor

Main Step 8: Present Project Results

Here we present the result of the study to the project board for approval or revision.

No	Task	Deliverable	Technique	Tool
8.1	Draft Report	End Report		Word Processor
8.2	Review Report	Quality Review		Word Processor
8.3	Prepare Presentation	Presentation		Presentation Software
8.4	Present Project Results	Project Sign Off	Board Review Meeting	Word Processor

This could be followed by implementation projects, preferably using an evolutionary delivery of the solutions, according to a plan which will phase in the new solutions into the current organisation. The role of the Project Board stops at this point. The responsibility for the phasing in of the solutions lies with the process managers as the normal part of the change control.

CONCLUSIONS

We have reviewed a possible management approach for an on-going programme of change. The programme can be implemented through process improvement projects undertaken in series or in parallel. We have reviewed a set of generic phases giving the most general 'menu' from which the programme manager in charge of changes can tailor a plan appropriate to each situation.

Chapter 6

Management Architecture

INTRODUCTION

In this chapter we shall relate the mission and objectives of the organisation to the design of its processes. We will see how we can formulate this mission and these objectives in a way which helps us to find out the true core processes that the organisation needs. We shall then try to understand the essence of management - in process terms - and to derive the bare bones of with what the strategic and tactical management should be concerned. Finally we shall outline some of the generic activities which support strategic and tactical management.

EXPRESSING THE MISSION

The notions of mission, goal and objectives are distinct ones but often confused. For example, a chemical company put out the following so-called 'mission statement':

> *'Our mission is to achieve 5% market share by year 2000, by being the preferred quality supplier to our industrial customers'*

In practice, the company was taken over by a larger group shortly after issuing the statement. The new group achieved immediately over 10% of the market. It seemed that the company immediately lost their mission! Yet the fact that they had something to offer was the reason why it was taken over. What changed after the take-over, was its objectives, not its goals.

If we try to understand the intentions of that company from an expression like '... a preferred quality supplier to our industrial customers ', we need to understand the reasoning in the mind of the executives who wrote the 'mission' statement, which was lost in the translation into words (see Figure 6.1).

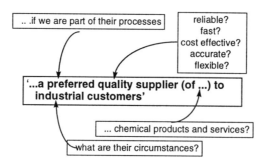

Figure 6.1 Analysing the Mission Statement

The *mission* is the reason why the organisation exists — the type of service or product that it offers to its customers. To make money is not a mission, except in the very rare case of a capital-holding company which buys and sells other companies in order to optimise the bottom line of its annual report. Even for such an investment company, the mission is not to make money but to provide a service to its customers. The profit (or loss) is the measurement of *how well* an organisation achieves its objectives, it is not an end in itself.

This simple truth has been recently rediscovered by management advisers looking at successful companies. James Heskett and his colleagues from the Harvard Business School, for example, found that a string of service companies including Southwest Airline, Taco Bell, MCI, Banc One and Intuit Corporation, realised the value of the 'Service-Profit Chain' by showing the relationship between profitability and customer loyalty and employee satisfaction — 'putting "hard" values on "soft" measures' (Heskett et al 1994).

The mission statement of our chemical company should therefore have reflected the end result it was aiming for, such as:

'To be a quality supplier of chemical products to industrial customers'

Goals

The *goals* of the organisation should qualify the mission into its sub-clauses and contain no more measurement or time scale than the mission itself.

For example, the goals of our chemical company, might be expressed as:

> 'To be a preferred quality supplier to our customers by:
>
> - providing value for money;
>
> - delivering that value-added sooner;
>
> - delivering that value-added more cost effectively than our competitors'

As a guideline, we could consider what our organisation means for our stakeholders. In his book *The Empty Raincoat*, Charles Handy suggests that there are six types of stakeholders (see Figure 6.7): the customers, the employees, the suppliers, the community (the surrounding environment), the shareholders and society as a whole (Handy 1994). Attention to the 'society' stockholder has been more prominent in recent years in the more ecologically aware organisations. The objective here is to reduce the impact on the environment due to the operation of the organisation.

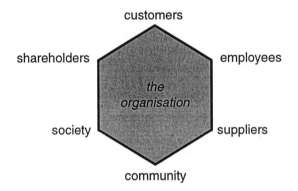

Figure 6.2 The Hexagon of the Stakeholders of an Organisation

Stakeholders

Eckart Wintzen is the Founder and Chairman of BSO, one of the largest systems houses in Europe, which is based in Holland. He has created a company where employees are happy (I was one of them some years ago). From a process engineering point of view, BSO was also an early example of a decentralised, 'flat' company where the policy of 'subsidiarity' has been the recipe for growth from day one, through the empowering of employees in small self-contained operational 'cells'.

Consistent with the awareness for a wide circle of stakeholders, the annual report of BSO always includes an environment balance sheet showing the cost of the environment effects caused by the company — including the cost of energy and resources (electricity, paper) and the evaluated cost which would be necessary for reducing the gas emissions (from heating, electricity generation, road traffic, air traffic and waste incineration) and the wastes (water and solids and dust). BSO calculated that the net cost per employee represented 954 Guilders (about $250) in 1991, and showed a decrease over the previous year.

ICI, the world chemical giant, also publishes an annual environmental report showing achievements against four main objectives: compliance to the most demanding standards; quantified reduction of wastes (e.g. 50% of 1990 figures by 1995); quantified energy and resource conservation; and recycling of its own products.

Balanced Scorecard

Robert Kaplan and David Norton from the Harvard Business School coined the phrase *Balanced Scorecard* for a set of considerations directed at financial and non-financial objectives (Kaplan and Norton 1992 and 1993). They argue that purely financial objectives and measurements often give a wrong picture of the actual position and health of an organisation. They suggest that the objectives should include four perspectives: financial; customer; innovation and learning; internal. These relate closely to considering the perspective of the stakeholders as customer, employees and shareholders. The 'internal business' expresses the need to have the required capability — that we treat as a tactical consideration rather than a strategic one.

The example of the mission statement of the chemical company I used earlier addresses the consideration for customers, but the statement could be enlarged to include, as a minimum, employee and shareholder goals, such as:

> *'To be a fair opportunity employer, encouraging our employees to show and develop their competency'*
>
> *'To sustain a profitable return for our investors'*

Key Performance Indicators (KPIs)

Having too many KPIs can be confusing and defeats the need for focusing the attention on the key considerations. One or two KPIs for each consideration is sufficient.

Examples of a KPI would be: 'number of defects per installed systems'; 'consumer complaints per 1000 passengers'; passengers per employee'; employees per aircraft'; 'customer loyalty as the number of repeat orders'; and 'Return on Investment'. In our example of a chemical company, a KPI might be: the 'rate of growth and retention of new customer' - which eventually results into 'market share'. Robert Kaplan and David Norton provide some suggestions for KPIs related to the four categories of objectives in their 'Balanced Scorecard' approach:

1) *Financial perspective*:

- return on capital employed
- cash flow
- profitability
- sales volume

2) *Customer perspective*:

- market share

- pricing index

- customer ranking survey

- customer satisfaction

3) *Innovation and learning perspective*:

- awarded patents

- new products introduced to the market

- qualifications obtained by employees

- marketable improvements to processes

4) *Internal perspective*:

- retention of staff

- degree of sharing of common culture and goals

- effective management of issues

Each organisation will have to decide what is important for them and, in doing so, will document what makes the difference between them and their competitors.

In qualifying the goals of our chemical company, say, we could formulate quantitative objectives as KPIs that define how much, how many, and by when? For example:

> *'Our objective is to achieve 5% of the market by year 2000, and 12% by year 2010'*

Mission, Goals and Objectives: Summary

The mission is the direction chosen by an organisation — the route in that direction is the chosen *strategy*, the milestones along the route are the *objectives*, the instruments for speed and mileage monitoring the progress along the road are the KPIs.

The relationship between mission, goals and objectives is illustrated informally in Figure 6.3.

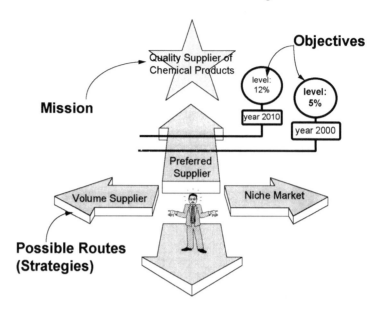

Figure 6.3 Mission, Goal and Strategy

A more formal diagram could help us to visualise these notions and their relationships. Figure 6.4 shows such a diagram, using a notation for concept diagrams which will be explained in Chapter 9.

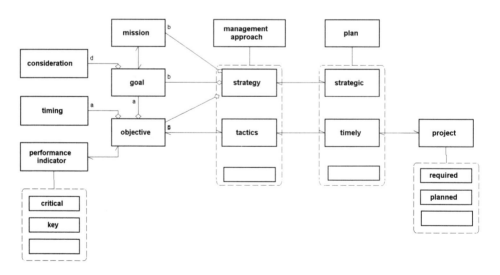

Figure 6.4 Concepts in Strategy and Tactics

CORE PROCESSES

Value analysis is the technique used to break down the outcome of a process into its main constituents and to define the process capabilities. We shall review this technique in Part III.

Core Capabilities

The core processes are those which deliver the core capabilities required by the organisation to meet its goals (see Figure 6.5). Everything else does not add any value. There is no need to make a difference between operational and support processes. This distinction is not consistent with our process approach. If we find that a process is needed but is not identified as a core process, then we must ask ourselves two questions:

1) *Is the process not really part of one of the core processes?* For example, procurement is often considered a 'support function', but is it not part of the core process 'providing the physical resources needed required by the organisation in the agreed form and at the best possible terms and conditions'?

2) *Is our mission really what we think it is?* Should we include what we are doing in what appears to be a support or accessory function? For example, 'offering a repair service to outside customers in addition to repairing our own vehicles' changes the mission of the repair shop.

To implement the core processes in the physical set-up of the organisation, we might, for convenience of place or people administration, create support divisions. However, we must remember that these divisions participate in the core processes we have identified in this model and that the management of the people and other resources in these 'support' divisions is distinct from the management of the core processes for the benefit of the organisation as a whole.

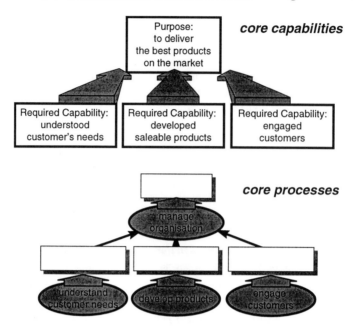

Figure 6.5 From Core Capabilities to Core Processes

The value analysis of the chemical company in our example would result in the diagram shown on Figure 6.6.

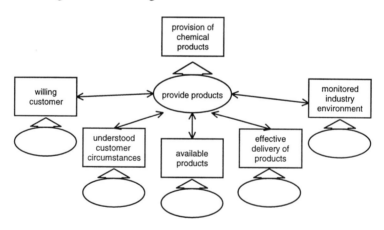

Figure 6.6 Core Capabilities of a Chemical Company

The identification and monitoring of the performance of the core processes is the role of the *Direction Management Process (DMP)* which manages the outcome of the organisation. This is a concept and a term used by the National Building Society for the re-engineering of their management structure (O'Brien and Wainwright 1993). It is the role of DMP to identify and create new core processes if necessary.

MANAGEMENT PROCESSES

Although every organisation has a large number of layers of management, the minimum number required from a process design point of view is only three (see Figure 6.7). These layers address respectively:

1) the management of the *direction*: managing the overall mission and objectives of the organisation;

2) the management of the *capabilities*: putting in place the required capabilities required to sustain the direction;

3) the management of the available *capabilities* for the actual doing - the *operation* itself.

Management Considerations

These three levels of consideration correspond to the traditional distinction between strategy, tactics, resources.

As we have seen, the difference between strategy and tactics is often confused. In this discussion, we shall make a clear distinction between them. Strategy is be the management approach concerned with mission, goals and quantified objectives (the 'WHAT'). A clear strategy leads to the identification of the capabilities required for achieving the goals and objectives (see Figure 6.7).

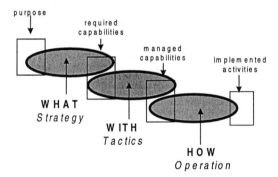

Figure 6.7 Generic Management Considerations

Tactics is the management approach concerned with developing and putting in place the required capabilities (the 'WITH'). They are concerned with planning the capabilities and making them available to the organisation.

Interdependency of Processes

There are clear differences in scope and activities between these different 'levels' of considerations, but we should not assume that one level is above the other. The spirit of process redesign is to understand the interdependencies of these processes, not to support any type of 'hierarchy'. Hierarchy is a notion which could be relevant to the management of people but does not belong to our process architecture.

Figure 6.8 shows the three main generic management processes: DMP; Capability Management Process (CMP); and Operation Management Process (OMP). There can only be one DMP because there is only one mission, but there are usually several CMPs, one for each of the required core capabilities. We shall identify the required capabilities at enterprise level with the core capabilities, delivered by the core processes.

In our example of a chemical company, the core CMPs would be:

1) *marketing*: generate willing customers;

2) *selling*: understand customer circumstances (and processes);

3) *production*: make the products (and services) available;

4) *delivery*: deliver products (and services) effectively;

5) *monitoring*: keep a watch on the industry environment (e.g. regulations) and monitor the standard of products and service.

Activities in Processes

Each process is implemented through well-defined activities. Even the Management Processes have well-defined activities. For example, we shall see that DMP includes planning, sharing understanding and direction, monitoring performance and managing change. In Figure 6.7, an ellipse represents a management process or an operational process (an activity). What is delivered by one process is a resource for the process at another level of consideration: DMP 'delivers' the mission (and everything implied by the concept of mission) and defines and uses a set of capabilities, each of which are 'delivered' by the corresponding CMP.

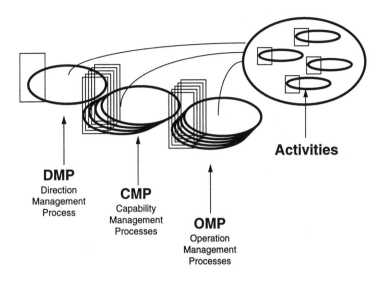

Figure 6.8 Generic Management Processes

We must be careful to separate in our mind the 'logical' management requirements from the organisational constraints; such as the size, the diversity or the geographical constraints imposed by the physical nature of the organisation. For example, we may have to group several activities at a given location into manageable units or the sheer size of an operation might require the creation of sub-divisions, which then need to be co-ordinated.

THE STRATEGIC AND TACTICAL PLANS

We have seen how the direction of the organisation is expressed in the form of mission, goals and objectives. The next step is to plan the capabilities — the processes and resources — required to achieve the objectives. In doing so, we shall also take into account the culture and the values of the organisation.

To be consistent with our understanding of mission, goals and objectives, the management approaches and plans should be as follows:

Strategic Plan

The preparation and production of the strategic plan is the role of DMP. The strategic plan is the documentation of the mission and the direction of the organisation, of 'WHAT' it delivers, of its 'raison d''être'. The Strategic Plan is used to identify and define the core capabilities that the organisation needs — the 'WITH' of the organisation.

Tactical Plan

The preparation and production of the strategic plan is the role of CMPs. It is a plan for implementing the tactics, typically over one year, and contains a statement of the qualifiers of the required capabilities: quantitative attributes of benefits and constraints — quality, cost and time scale (the 'WHEN'). The tactical plans are often called the *strategies* (with a small 's').

Businesses and some public services have adopted the practice of producing an annual report. This report often includes, in fact or in spirit, a form of strategic plan, elements of a tactical plan as well as financial and operational data.

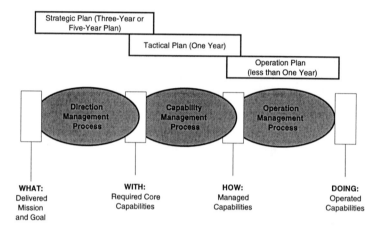

Figure 6.9 Management Processes and Plans

In the following sections, we shall outline some generic activities of the DMP and CMPs.

GENERIC ACTIVITIES IN DIRECTION MANAGEMENT PROCESS

In this section, we shall describe some of the generic activities which could be included in the design of a DMP. We shall use a simplified version of the notation for the activities, which will be fully explained in Part IV.

The main types of activity corresponding to the considerations addressed by DMP are shown in Figure 6.10:

1) *define the mission, goals and objectives*: the strategic direction of the organisation, closely associated with understanding the needs of customers and the market;

2) *initiate and manage changes:* steer the organisation through the changes and sustain those changes by identifying and describing the capabilities that the organisation must have;

3) *assess achievements*: monitor the impact of internal and external events or issues;

4) *share direction*: the common purposes such as mission, goals and objectives involving stakeholders inside and outside the organisation.

> The overall documentation of these considerations is the strategic plan.

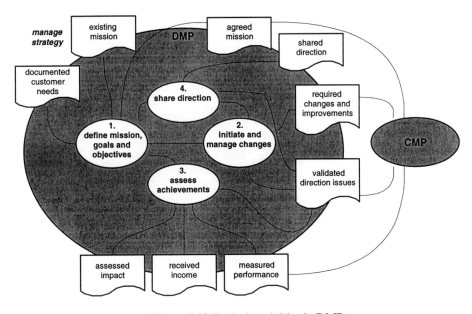

Figure 6.10 Typical Activities in DMP

Later on in the book (Part IV), we shall define what we expect to find in an implementable process. In the case of the DMP we would identify a number of attributes for each of these activities including:

1) purpose and output (WHAT);

2) *measurements* of achievement and quality (qualification of the delivered output);

3) *what is* required from other activities (WITH);

4) own capabilities (HOW): there is usually a one-to-one correspondence between own capabilities and activities;

5) roles in the team: all the roles in the DMP activities.

GENERIC ACTIVITIES IN A CAPABILITY MANAGEMENT PROCESS

Each CMP manages one of the core capabilities specified by DMP. Each of these CMPs would have a number of activities, some generic and some specific. We can use a diagram (see Figure 6.11) to show these generic activities and their relationships with DMP's activities (see Figure 6.11).

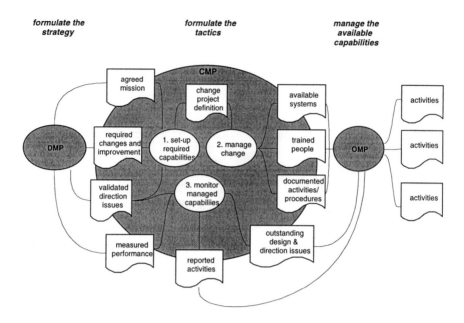

Figure 6.11 Generic Activities in CMPs

The main activities corresponding to the considerations addressed by a CMP are

1) *set-up the required capabilities*: put in place the management framework and define the process design and implementation projects;

2) *manage change programme*: initiate and manage the implementation projects;

3) *monitor the capabilities*: managed by the Operation Management Processes.

The capabilities made available by a CMP are managed by OMPs and 'enacted' in activities by people using the available *logistical means* such as information and communication systems, buildings and transport.

CONCLUSIONS

The understanding of the mission in terms of the required capabilities will enable us to design the required management and operational processes. However, it is very rare that designers work on a brand new organisation. The more common requirement is to setup a programme of change providing the framework in which new or existing processes will be carved out from the existing organisation. It is totally impractical to freeze the operation for a while in order to design a new one.

What is more realistic is to sustain an on-going climate of improvements, taking care to comply with the culture of the organisation and with its natural reluctance to change. The management teams are responsible for settingup and maintaining the processes which will manage these unavoidable changes.

A possible road map for on-going improvements was outlined in Part I. In the next chapters we shall review the techniques for understanding and designing the OMPs.

———————————— Part III
Value Analysis Applied to Processes

—————————————————— Chapter 7

Introduction to Value Analysis

INTRODUCTION

The notion of value used in *a*BC*d* is derived from the design of products to provide a powerful *Value Analysis* technique for understanding the underlying logic of processes and for defining precisely their outputs and necessary inputs. Value Analysis will be used to produce a logical model of the enterprise or system which is *non-redundant*: a process will appear only once in the model, with all its relevant concepts, business objects, events and roles. The model is the foundation for the definition of the activities, roles and logistic resources which can then be implemented in the reality of the business.

A benefit of the rigorous approach is that the results are reuseable across the enterprise as a whole - the same logic applies to all the parts of the implemented process, even though the parts may be implemented quite differently.

THE CONCEPT OF VALUE

Value can be a very emotive and fuzzy notion. Like quality, everyone has a private definition for it. For the purpose of process design we need to introduce a more formal and precise definition.

The notion of value is used in the design of industrial products, where the shape of the product is determined by its function. In this, 'value' is classified as either *use value* (the ability to achieve the function) or *esteem value* (the status or regard associated with ownership).

Value Analysis in industrial product design is a cost reduction technique which seeks to identify and eliminate the unnecessary components by the analysis of its functions (Miles 1972). The techniques were invented in the USA at the end of World War II and are widely used in Europe (Adams 1987).

Value Chain vs. Value Model

This Value Analysis technique considered here centres on the value of the end-product delivered by a process, value which determines the 'shape' of the process from the function that it needs to assume. This employs a different notion of 'value' from the approach to the improvement of business processes popularised by Professor Michael Porter of the Harvard Business School in his analysis of 'value chains' (Porter 1985). Although Porter clearly identifies the role of the value added by a process for the benefit of its customers, the application of his value-added chain is often reduced to a desirable attribute - or set of attributes -, usually cost attributes, which relates to the output of a process. The object of the improvement is to maximise or minimise this attribute throughout the chain of activities. The performance of each element of the chain of activities is considered and the value is measured as a numerical value of the performance of the process. This is valuable for optimising an existing process but does not give us the means of challenging the way it is designed, the reason for the existence of the activities carried out.

Performing Value Analysis concentrates the mind on the effectiveness of a process whereas looking at the Value Chain is relevant when we want to improve its efficiency.

Value in Processes

> In designing processes, we shall define *value* as an element of the end-product expressing a *capability* provided to its user.

The user can be a person, an organisation or more generally another process.

Figure 7.1 Capability is a Resource Needed in a Particular State
(© Jim Cooper Graphics)

For example, an end-product could be 'a validated order' or 'an appliance in a state of readiness'. More abstract capabilities could be for example: 'an agreed requirement'; 'a confirmed customer need'; 'a shared understanding', where 'agreed', 'confirmed' and 'shared' have a very precise meaning in terms of what the end-product is for.

This approach enables us to challenge an existing process as it is implemented by working backwards from the end-product. The Value Analysis technique summarised in Figure 7.2 consists of:

- understanding the purpose of the end-product,

- deriving the capability that it provides,

- understanding the components of that capability — the concepts which are necessary and sufficient for defining these capabilities,

- and the states of these entities which are relevant to the process.

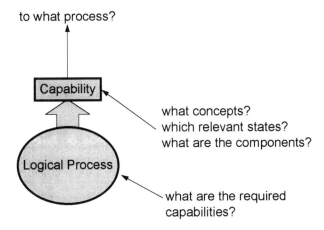

Figure 7.2 End-Product as a Capability

Engineers will recognise that Value Analysis in product design also rests on these basic considerations. In the next sections we shall formalise the steps and notations relevant to process design. This approach can be applied to a whole organisation: the definition of its mission and goals can be expressed as delivering value to its customer. It is also possible to apply it to the most humble of its processes. Size is irrelevant.

Value Models

With Value Analysis, we can produce a formal model of:

1) the business direction and objectives requirement (the WHAT);

2) the details of the process itself and its sub-processes (the HOW),

3) the format of the specification of the required capabilities and abstract resources (the WITH), the people and logistics;

4) the formal basis of the information systems, the definition of the entities and IT processes required for supporting the business processes.

If an Object Oriented (OO) development method is followed, the Value Analysis provides the definition of the 'business objects' required by the system developers.

This model should be justified and logically demonstrated. There is fortunately a well-established body of mathematical theory which is directly relevant to our purpose. It is not necessary to be a mathematician to apply the technique described in this chapter, but the fact that this formal basis exists gives confidence that it will produce well-constructed models.

The theory was developed by the mathematicians and philosophers Bertrand Russell and Alfred North Whitehead at the beginning of this century. It includes a formal definition of sets and types (Whitehead and Russell 1910 and Russell 1956) and was applied originally to process modelling by mathematician John Edwards who was at the time employed by a commercial organisation for database and systems development (Edwards 1984), He was also a member of the ISO committee dealing with research on a conceptual framework for database design (Griethuysen and King 1985). He realised that it was necessary to understand the logic of the process where these systems and data were used before attempting to design the IT systems. In formalising that work, he proposed Ptech (Process Technology), one of the forerunners of the application of the object paradigm to the domain of business processes and automation. The Value Analysis technique recommended in this book for aBCd integrates the work of Edwards into a complete BPR approach.

In the following discussion, we shall sometimes refer to 'concept types', 'entity types' or 'event types' to remind designers that they should carefully separate the generic from the particular. For example, when we discuss 'invoice' as a concept type, we shall mean the thing 'invoice' in general in the context of the process under study, but not a particular invoice, such as 'invoice number 1235 for a computer system model AZ999'. We can think of a type as a class of things and this enables us to discuss the property of the abstract class and not specific instances, delaying implementation issues to a further stop of the design. So in Value Analysis we are modelling a concept, an entity or an event in an abstract, generic sense.

Normalised Models

The non-redundant approach we follow also results in a model in which a given logical process will be found only once. This useful property is also known as *normalisation*. When we are considering a logical process, all its aspects can be considered at once. This gives us the confidence that we are not forgetting something in our discussion and that we can describe the process completely. For example, if we are considering the process of issuing an invoice, many different departments might issue invoices, for different types of services or goods. However, all the aspects of the generic 'invoice issuing process' will be found at only one place in the model and can be developed and maintained in a more consistent fashion. This overcomes problems caused by the common practice in system design of starting from scratch every time a department needs an invoice handling application, which results in the procedures, systems and data structures becoming incompatible.

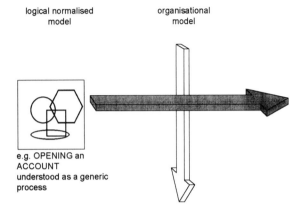

Figure 7.3 The Logical Process Model

We have seen in Chapter 3 that we can view an enterprise or a complex system from different points of view: the organisational, the logical, the physical and the informational. Value Analysis is the technique which enables us to understand and document the logical point of view. So the result of Value Analysis is a normalised logical model of the processes under study and includes the concept types, entity types and event types for these processes (see Figure 7.3).

OVERVIEW OF VALUE MODELLING

A Value Analysis model takes the form of three types of diagrams (see Figure 7.4):

- the *Value-Added Diagram (VAD)*, used to represent the value contents of a capability, supporting the capability architecture;

- the *Concept Diagram (CD)*, supporting the concept analysis; and

- the *Event Diagram (ED)* showing the state of the entities, used to model the event analysis.

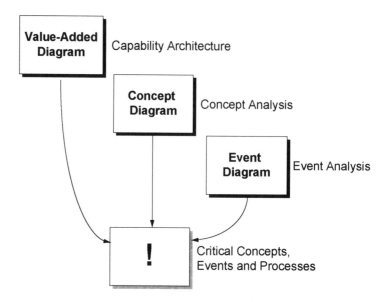

Figure 7.4 The Three Complementary Models in Value Analysis

The modelling of the capabilities allows the definition of the framework - the *architecture* - of the logical processes. It shows the decomposition of the logical processes and their relationship. This is based on a simple but formal notion of exchange of capabilities in which a logical process adds value to its inputs in delivering its end-product.

The *Concept Analysis* analysis formalises the concepts used in each process and between processes, as well as their relationships. This is the *static* model of the relevant concepts in each process which embody the semantics, the meaning that we attach to the concepts in a given context.

The *Event Analysis* analysis is derived from the Concept Analysis and expresses the *dynamic* behaviour of the concepts, the processes: the triggering conditions, the exceptions and the side-effects.

From the three models, it is possible to derive the concept and the event which are critical to the processes. We shall see later on how to express them.

REUSEABLE COMPONENTS

It is easier to understand and describe the links which exist between processes if the model is normalised (non-redundant) as we just described. This is an important advantage of having to produce an abstract model of processes first. The components of the processes are likely to be reuseable without modification, whereas the implemented components of the organisation — the physical and observable activities — are the way they are because of other considerations in terms of business or geographical constraints.

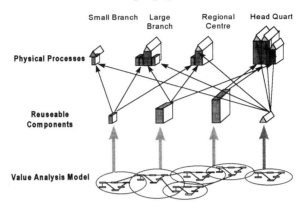

Figure 7.5 Reuseable Logical Components

In building our abstract logical model we effectively manufacture the building blocks with which we can construct the physical processes at the various places in the organisation, taking into account the local business situation and constraints (see Figure 7.5).

RESILIENCE TO CHANGES

Value Analysis deliberately avoids any aspects concerning physical implementation of the processes of a system, including timing, volume and location data. The process architecture is the foundation for the specification of the resources, activities, people and logistical means which will be deployed within the business constraints of geography and organisation (see Figure 7.6).

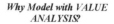

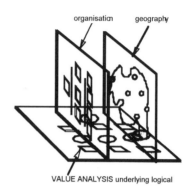

Figure 7.6 The Underlying Value Model

Value Analysis models deliver neither the physical implementation of the processes nor the infrastructure of an organisation or system. These are considered in the other views of the enterprise (organisational and physical). The complete specification of the resources would also include the physical constraints such as volumes, timing, location, platforms. The design of information systems in particular can proceed from the foundation laid down as the process architecture.

The independence of the Value Analysis model from both the internal structure of an organisation and any geographical distribution of that organisation is a major reason for its resilience to change. The model validity would typically span decades or more, whereas the system or organisation might change weekly or monthly.

TEAM MODELLING

Value Analysis is typically used in participative sessions in which a trained facilitator works with a team to elicit the underlying common structures of the organisation, system or processes. The result of the sessions is typically handled by a process designer. The main task of the process designer is to produce a formal and consistent description of the logic of the processes. The use of a software tool becomes quickly necessary in order to cope with the size of the models which are generated.

The constant requirement put on the designers to uncover the abstract logic of the processes has a beneficial side-effect: it leads to non-redundant models which can be worked on independently by different teams, or by the same team on different parts at different times. The various contributions can be consolidated into a single model if necessary.

CONCLUSIONS

The Value Analysis technique is used to produce a normalised, formally consistent logical model of the enterprise or system.

Applying a rigorous approach leads to results which are more resilient to the business or technological environment. The results are templates reuseable across the enterprise as a whole, even though the parts may be implemented quite differently when local conditions and constraints are taken into account.

The next chapter describes in more detail the concepts and notations of the three modelling techniques we have introduced.

Chapter 8

Value-Added Modelling

OVERVIEW

Value-Added modelling takes a logical view of the processes within an organisation or system by ignoring the physical structure and implementation of the organisation or system under study. This means that the model produced is independent of any current or envisaged future implementation of these processes. It generates a normalised model within which each isolated process is understood in relationship to the overall model.

The model helps to manage and reduce the complexity of the study by isolating processes and sub-processes. Because the model is normalised, each part can be studied with the confidence that we are not forgetting or duplicating something, and that there will not be conflicts with other parts developed independently. We can also start at any point and refine the model towards more detailed levels (*top-down*) or towards more general or broader levels (*bottom-up*). However, if possible, it is faster and more systematic to start from the ultimate mission of the organisation or the system and to work top-down.

VALUE-ADDED DIAGRAM

The basic notation of the Value Analysis includes *processes* adding value to one or more *products*, which are its resources, in order to deliver a single *end-product*. When we model, we can use the term *product* to designate what is produced or used by a process, although it could also be termed a 'capability'. The example shown in Figure 8.1 is a simple Value-Added Diagram of a vending machine.

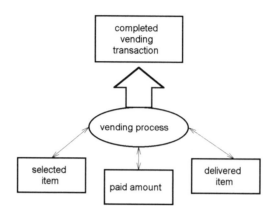

Figure 8.1 Value-Added Diagram of a Vending Machine

The product of one process may be the resource of another. The double ended arrow in Figure 8.1 indicates that a process *uses* a product.

An end-product represents the value added by a process. The end-product could be expressed as one of a number of concepts, such as:

- a deliverable service;
- a function;
- a mission or purpose;
- a goal or objective;
- a need;
- a deliverable product.

An end-product implies a commitment to deliver a product in a particular state (see Figure 8.2).

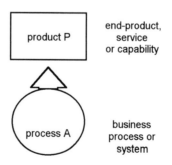

Figure 8.2 Basic Principle of Value Analysis

Each process has only one end-product and a given end-product is delivered by only one process. Experience shows that if we identify several end-products for a process, this is the indication that we have not completed the conceptual analysis of that end-product and that we must find the concept which encompasses all the apparently different products.

THE CUSTOMER PROCESS

The end-product is always for the benefit of a customer. The customer may be a true customer, external to the organisation modelled, or an internal customer within the organisation or another process. The customer will be modelled as a logical process (see Figure 8.3).

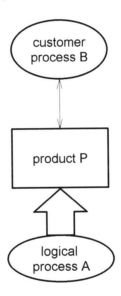

Figure 8.3 The Customer of a Process

There is no other type of relationship between a process and its customer. Therefore, an end-product defines completely the interface between the two logical processes; the *producer* and the *customer*. A Concept Type Diagram (that we shall see in detail later on) will be the formal description of that product.

All the communications and the physical exchanges are completely defined by what the product is. The model yields a protocol of communication between processes A and B. The protocol could be as follows (see Figure 8.4):

- process B requests from process A a product P;

- processes A and B agrees the particular shape, status, delay and cost - in other words 'state' of the required product;

- process A commits to the delivery;

- process B may supply money or other resources to A for completing the transaction;

- the exchange takes place;

- all the consequences and loose ends are resolved (for example, delivery notes, invoices, legal commitments).

A product defines completely the interface between two logical processes. A product represents the complete set of transactions between them. This is a simple but powerful corollary of the definitions introduced so far. A product is usually a complex thing and could be described in its own Concept and Event models (that we shall discuss in the next chapters).

The notation makes clear that there is only one product from one process (single thick arrow) and that a customer process may use the product (thin arrow). A double arrow indicates that there is usually a dialogue, such as an exchange between customer and producer.

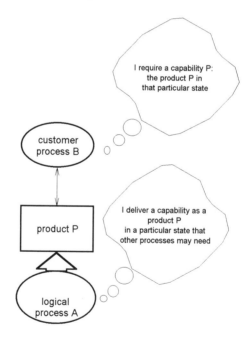

Figure 8.4 Interface Between Processes

It is important to note that the Value-Added Diagram is *not* a flow diagram. The links in Figure 8.4 (thin and fat arrows) indicate dependencies, relationships between process and products, which should be read as interfaces or channels operating in both directions; a process specifies what it needs and what it can provide through a relation (thin arrow) and it gets back its required capability from the relationship.

One process may need several products, provided by other processes (see Figure 8.5). A given product can be used by several processes.

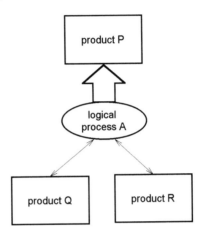

Figure 8.5 Products used by a Process

DOMAIN OF A PROCESS

Any logical process has a very well-defined view of the environment in which it operates. It can 'see' only its resource-product(s) and its end-product. The world of a logical process bound by the horizon of its resource-product(s) and its end-product is known as its 'domain' (see Figure 8.6). The logical process is totally unaware of all other products, resources and processes beyond its domain, and cannot directly affect or be affected by any of them.

If during our analysis, we need to consider some interaction with a process which is not connected through an already defined interface, then this indicates that the model needs to be revised to include additional products as interfaces.

Any one logical process is not affected by a change in any other logical process, unless that change is taken into account in the interface between the processes.

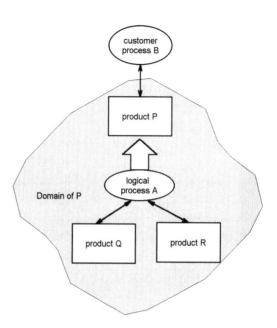

Figure 8.6 Domain of a Process

A *process*, its *end-product* and its *resource-products* together constitute the *domain* of a process. The Value-Added Diagram serves as a framework - an architecture for the processes and their products. This strict separation of concerns is a powerful technique of simplification, and is a key feature of Value Analysis. The model hides the complexity of the interfaces which determine how a process gets what it needs and how it provides what is needed from it. Hidden behind the products are both the detailed definition and the temporal or synchronisation aspects of the interface. Products are usually complex concepts. For example, 'a satisfied customer requirement' implies at least two concepts: 'a known customer requirement' and 'an offered service', which are themselves complex concepts.

INTERNAL VIEW OF A PROCESS

The more detailed levels of a process can be modelled in the same way as the overall process, provided that the end-product is the product of one of the sub-processes and that each of the identified resource-products is used by one or several of the sub-processes (see Figure 8.7).

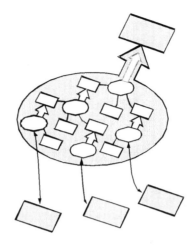

Figure 8.7 Modelling of the Sub-Processes

This detailed analysis can be repeated if necessary until we are able to describe the sub-processes with the required degree of precision (see Figure 8.8).

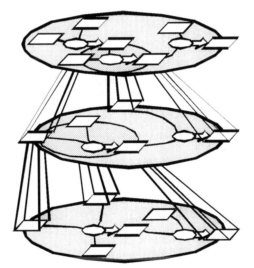

Figure 8.8 Levelling of the Value-Added Diagrams

The basis for detailing the logical processes at one level of abstraction is the domain. These more detailed processes themselves may be decomposed to yet lower levels of detail — down to the level of interest, required by the analyst. Not all domains will necessarily require decomposition. At a given level, some processes might be completely understood and need no further analysis.

RECEIVED RESOURCES

There are resources which are used by a process, but are not specified by that process. These resources are referred to as 'received' resources. Such received resources should only be included in the model if they are truly material to the task which a process is to carry out. We often include these resources at the beginning of the work but after further analysis we realise that their role is reduced and we eventually remove them from the model.

To express that products are 'received' by the process rather than 'used', a dotted arrow is employed. This is shown in Figure 8.9 where the received resource 'available office' is an example of a resource which can be taken for granted and is not a concern of the process currently being modelled (the 'sell service' does not add value to that particular resource).

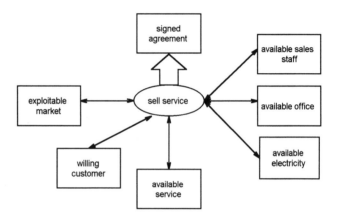

Figure 8.9 Received Resources

A more extreme example would be the provision of a resource 'available electricity', which is a vital asset to most processes, although most business people do not need to worry about it in modelling their business. But if we were modelling the activities of the system manager, this would become a critical resource, which is likely to be a 'used' rather than a 'given' resource.

BY-PRODUCTS

Products generated as an indirect consequence of a process can be modelled as '*by-products*', if they are of real significance to the process modelled. Again, what is of significance as a by-product is a matter of judgement and should be included only if used elsewhere (see Figure 8.10).

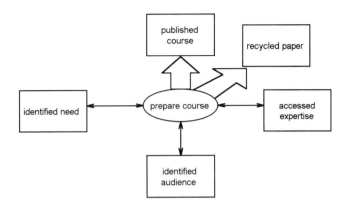

Figure 8.10 By-Products

For example, the waste paper generated in an office would not normally be of significance, but for a print room's operations the recycling of paper might be of interest and might require a specific, identified process. Some by-products may be of significance because of the extra effort or expense incurred in disposing of them.

STEPS IN BUILDING THE VALUE ANALYSIS ARCHITECTURE

The Value-Analysis Diagrams form the visible representation of the Value-Added Architecture, the blue print of the logical model. To draw them we need to consider at the same time the Concept and Event models of the domain under study. However, the approach, in broad terms, is as follows:

1) *identify what we want to do*: what mission, product or service is delivered to a customer (internal or external to the organisation);

2) *determine what we need to do it*: what are the capabilities, the necessary resources required by the single process in order to deliver its mission, product or service;

3) *establish how we do it*: which is the single process delivering the required product or service.

We always start from the end: clarifying the goal or end-product of the domain under study — the 'WHAT' of the domain — and proceed backwards to determine WITH what capability and HOW we will achieve it.

NAMING CONVENTIONS

The names of end-products or resource-products should always use a noun qualified with adjectives or participles that express the state of the product. For example: 'available service', validated application', 'maintained state of law and order' or 'discharged commitment'. By convention, the singular for the names of products is used because we are always considering the type of things: *'customer'* as a type, not *'a particular customer'* or *'customers'*.

The naming of processes is not critical to the integrity of the analysis. In fact the name of a process is often left out in the initial steps of the analysis. However, the following conventions will be applied to the naming of processes:

> A *process name* will be a *verb in the imperative tense*, expressing a command. For example: 'provide service', 'check application', 'deliver a policing service' or 'run operation'.

SUMMARY

The Value-Added model is an abstract, logical analysis of processes. Processes are analysed in terms of the capability that they deliver (their end result) and the capabilities required from other processes, independently of any particular implementation of the processes.

These logical processes can be reused across the organisation or system by means of abstraction and normalisation techniques. The Value-Added model promotes a reduction of the complexity and ease of understanding by decomposition, localisation of the concerns and hiding of details. This is achieved by following a simple but formal line of reasoning: processes have a precisely defined domain which includes themselves, their end-product and their resources - but having no knowledge of other processes.

Processes can be analysed from high levels of generality down to lower, more detailed levels, independent of physical implementation.

Chapter 9

Concept Modelling

INTRODUCTION

Behind everything we do there is a concept. The ability to form concepts is what arguably distinguishes human beings from the other animals. This is especially true in business. Every activity has, or used to have, a purpose and is the application of some concepts. However, when these underlying concepts have been forgotten or corrupted, as they often have, the sense of the activities being undertaken is often lost. Edward de Bono goes even further and proposes that organisations should have a Concept Research & Development Department for creating and developing the concepts which will eventually give prosperity to that organisation (de Bono 1993). In his book *Sur/Petition*, he discusses the implications and consequences of understanding the role of concepts in the success of enterprises. In this book, we shall see how we can clarify and formalise the concepts in an organisation and translate them into processes.

As process designers, our first task is to rediscover or clarify these concepts. We shall be helped in this task by the Concept Type modelling explained in this chapter.

CONCEPTS

Concepts are a representation of our knowledge of reality from our particular point of view. There is therefore no such thing as a concept outside its context. This is why the capability architecture introduced in the previous chapter is an essential framework for reasoning about business processes or systems.

If we want to talk about a business reality, such as an invoice for some goods, there are a number of physical and intangible things which together constitute what we mean by an invoice. These can be expressed from a number of viewpoints (see Figure 9.1).

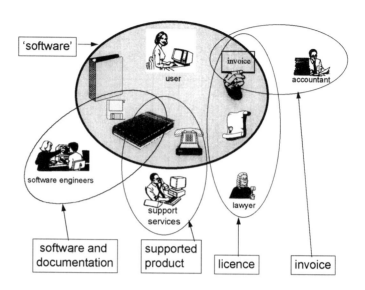

Figure 9.1 Concepts are Representations of Reality

For example, from the software engineer's point of view a product consists only of the code, the documentation and the media. From the support services' perspective, however, the behaviour and usage of the product as described in the user manual are the only relevant concepts of the product. When we model processes, we must have clear in our mind which perspectives are relevant.

We do not analyse what to do every time we dress or wash or cross a road. We perform these actions whatever the circumstances or the country we are in, without really thinking about them because we have in our mind 'patterns' or thoughts acquired through experience or education. A *concept* is an abstraction of the set of thoughts sharing a common characteristic.

What we are doing is defining a '*type*' of thing that we can treat as a single object. Formal discussions of these issues can be found in the literature about the theory of sets (Russell 1956) or in the most formal discussions on object-oriented data design (Edwards 1984, Odell 1989).

Entity is a more common term than 'concept'; entities are anything of interest whereas concepts are the things which are pure creation of the mind. The techniques discussed here apply to the most generic 'entities'. However, in process design it is easier to talk about concepts in the context of processes and activities because concepts are what underpin our purposeful activities. For that reason, in the following we shall use the term '*concepts*' to mean the same thing as '*entity type*'.

Abstraction is what allows us to deal with commonalities between groups of things, ignoring detailed irrelevant differences in the context under consideration. We can abstract from reality by one of three approaches (see Figure 9.2):

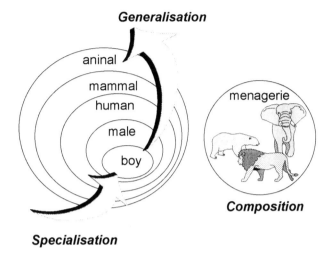

Figure 9.2 Abstraction Techniques

1) *classification*: grouping according to defined rules or characteristics, for example male or female, sometimes called specialisation because we assign a concept to a sub-type;

2) *generalisation*: discovering what a group of things has in common, for example motor car, a bicycle and a motorbike are 'vehicles'; this involves effectively finding general rules or characteristics from instances in order to identify the super-type of concepts;

3) *composition*: describing a collection of objects as a single thing for which a rule or characteristic is not obvious to formulate - for example a software product which could include the code of the program, the media, the licence, the manual, the test data, the box and the support service.

Naming of Concepts

Concepts are designated by *nouns*. Because a concept is always a set of things, we shall always use the singular: 'person', 'invoice' (unless the plural is the only grammatically acceptable form as in 'securities'). This convention applies not only to concepts, but also to sub-types, states, partitions and roles. A noun can be preceded, if appropriate, by qualifying adjectives and participles: 'available and validated requirement'.

CONCEPT MODELLING

Concept modelling is concerned with the analysis of the concepts relevant to a logical process and their relationships to other processes. In this chapter, we consider only the static aspects of concepts. The dynamic relationships in a process: how a concept changes from one state to another and events and precedence rules between events will be considered in the next chapter.

Process Domains

In the Value-Added modelling described in Chapter 8, we defined the domain of a logical process. With Concept modelling we are going to identify the concepts which give a meaning to what is going on within a domain and in relationship with other domains.

Each logical process has its own concept model and the scope of a concept model is the domain of a logical process (see Figure 9.3).

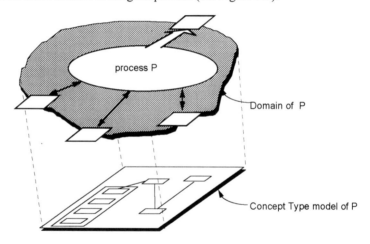

Figure 9.3 Concept Type Model of a Domain

Concept Types of an Interface

A notion of critical importance concerns the overlap of domains within a Value-Added model. In Chapter 8, we saw that the end-product of one process is usually the resource-product of another. A product encapsulates the interface between two processes. Since the same product figures in both of the overlapping domains, the two processes must share the concepts associated with this product (see Figure 9.4).

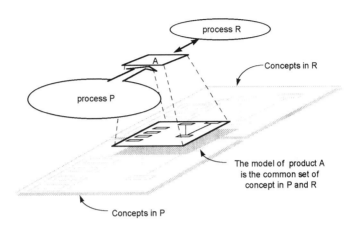

Figure 9.4 Shared Concept Types

In Figure 9.4, the concepts shared between processes P and R describe both the end-product of one and the resource-products of the other. They also define completely the protocol of the interface between the processes.

The links in a value-added diagram, connecting a process to its resource-products and to its end-product, do not represent flows of information but shared concepts.

The protocol of interaction between processes can be implemented in different ways, for example as a message transfer, a permanent database, or a physical exchange of documents, people or materials.

The use of a software facility (design workbench) for the modelling ensures the consistency between domains.

CONCEPT DIAGRAMS

Concept models take the form of *concept diagrams*. A summary of the notation can also be found in Chapter 15. Figure 9.5 illustrates a simple *concept diagram* for a 'financial service'.

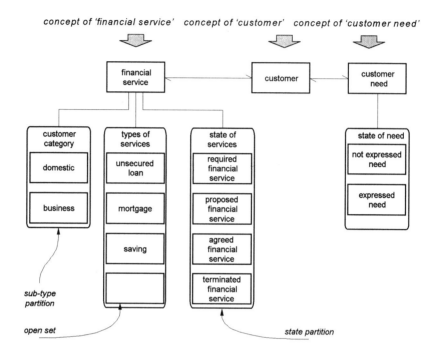

Figure 9.5 A Simple Concept Type Diagram - Financial Service

There are two types of *node* in such a diagram:

- *concept nodes*: a rectangle with the concept identifier written within;
- *partitions*: enclosing a number of concepts, as explained in the following sections.

Partitions on a Concept Diagram

Partitions are a way of expressing that a concept type can be sub-typed into smaller sets. For example, a 'financial service' can be an 'unsecured loan', a 'mortgage' or a 'saving' (see Figure 9.6).

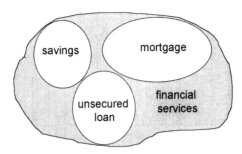

Figure 9.6 Sub-Types of Financial Services

These sub-types are totally independent and an instance of one cannot become an instance of another. If I sign up a mortgage with a financial organisation, say, I cannot change it into a saving. If I pay up more than the amount of the loan, I do not automatically start saving. A savings account is a completely different type of financial service, with different conditions and behaviour. We represent this analysis with a *sub-type partition* as shown on Figure 9.5.

A sub-type is also a concept in its own right, and may itself have partitions associated with it and participate in any other relationship type permitted for a concept.

The same concept can be partitioned in different ways. In our example, a financial service can be 'domestic' or 'business'. It is possible in this way to represent 'a required unsecured loan for a domestic customer' (see Figure 9.7). Or the concept 'person' might have sub-type partitioned into 'role' and 'sex', allowing a particular instance of a person to be identified as a 'male employee'. This is a powerful instrument for describing reality.

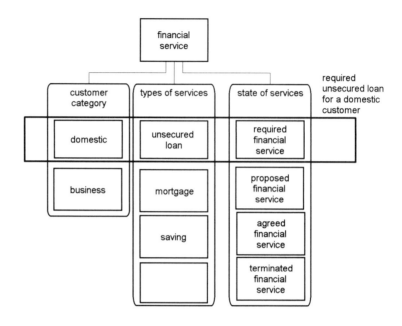

Figure 9.7 Multiple Sub-Typing

Each partition has its own rule used to assign a new concept to its sub-type. The rule can be explicit or implied. For example, to decide if a financial service is for a business, the applicant must provide a registered company identification. The name of the rule is written at the top of the partition box.

A concept in a partition can itself be sub-typed. The members of a partition inherit *all the properties* of their super-type. In addition they can have properties of their own.

State Partition

A financial service can also be sub-typed according to its state. For instance, an account can be 'required', proposed', 'agreed' or 'terminated'. A given account can also evolve from one state to another (but not two of these states simultaneously).

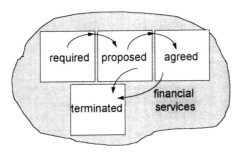

Figure 9.8 States of Financial Services

We represent this situation as a *state partition*, a dotted box enclosing the list of concept states, as shown on Figure 9.5.

Once classified in a sub-type partition, a Concept Type cannot be re-classified into a different sub-type of the same partition. But it can be re-classified into a different state in the same state partition, where only one state is permitted at a time.

Partition Rules

To summarise, there are two categories of partitioning or sub-set; the genuine *sub-type partition* of a concept and the *state partitions* that a concept can take. A new concept can be assigned to only one sub-type for the duration of its life. But a concept can be reassigned to one state or another - 'reclassified' - during its life. Sub-type partitions are drawn with a solid line whereas state partitions are shown as a dashed line.

The following rules apply to both categories of partitions.

1) The sub-types within a partition are mutually exclusive; any instance of the Concept Type must be of one, and only one, sub-type of the partition.

2) The partition is given a name which expresses the rule used to classify an instance into one of the sub-types, e.g. 'customer category'.

3) A sub-type partition may include a complete set of sub-types, identified by name. This is referred to as a closed set or a 'complete partition'.

4) A sub-type partition may also be an open set or an 'incomplete partition' where states of no concern to the domain are omitted but shown as an unnamed node as the last in the partition's list of sub-types. This is useful when all possible sub-types may not be of relevance to the modelling of the domain under study.

5) A concept may have any number of sub-type partitions associated with it. An instance of the concept will be sub-typed in each partition.

6) A concept may have more than one super-type. This concept inherits the property of all its super-types.

7) Because sub-types are always mutually exclusive, they may not 'overlap' - an instance of a type therefore cannot be simultaneously a member of two sub-types. For example, if an employee can be a salesperson and a manager, the concepts salesperson and manager cannot be sub-types of the same partition. The partitions of 'employee' in this case should be 'rank' (e.g. 'manager' and 'assistant') and 'role' (e.g. 'salesperson', 'administrator', 'stock manager').

Relationships Between Concepts

Partitions express a special category of relationship between concepts. There are three further possible categories of relationship as shown in Figure 9.9 and discussed in the next three subsections.

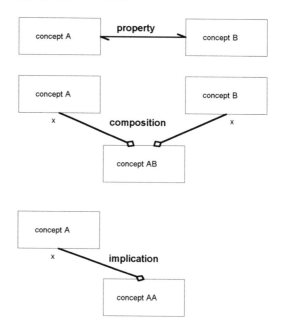

Figure 9.9 Relationships on a Concept Type Diagram

Property

A '*property*' is a relationship between two independent concepts which expresses that they are associated. For example, the concept 'financial service' may have a relationship with the concept 'customer' but each has independent existence and properties.

A property relationship is in fact made up of two relations connecting the concepts, one in each direction from a source to a target concept. This is expressed on the concept diagram by the shape of the *property link* — a line with a half arrow at each end (see Figure 9.9).

A *recursive property can also exist* between two concepts of the same types. For example, 'persons' can have a 'parent-child' relationship, or a 'husband-wife' relationship. This is indicated by a link relationship looping on the same concept (see Figure 9.10).

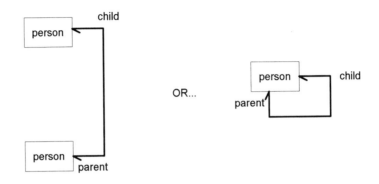

Figure 9.10 Model of Parenthood

Composition

A '*composition*' is a relationship used to show that a concept is made up of two or more other concepts. A composition is a form of 'made-of' relationship. In Figure 9.9 'AB' is shown to inherit from both 'A' and 'B'. Reading the relationship the other way around, we can say also that 'A' and 'B' are 'part of' 'AB'.

A motor car, for example, is made up of a chassis, an engine and four wheels. Although chassis, engine and wheel can have their own separate existence, a motor car is the sum of the parts. Another example is the concept of 'software product', which is composed of concepts 'manual', 'media' and 'licence'.

Composition relationships are indicated on the concept diagram by drawing a line between the composed concept and its components, with a diamond at the component end. The members of the same composition are identified by supplying the same name — usually a single letter — to each link in the relationship ('x' in the diagram on Figure 9.9).

Inheritance from more than one concept is referred to as '*multiple inheritance*'. In the example shown in Figure 9.11, a motor car can be considered as made of the concepts: chassis, engine and wheel (composition 'a'). But it is also composed of basic design and accessories concepts (composition 'b'). These are two different perspectives on the concept 'motor car'.

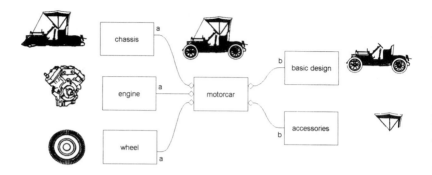

Figure 9.11 Multiple Inheritance

Implication

An *implication* is a special case of a composition where there is only one component. In Figure 9.9, one would say that 'A' implies 'AA' or 'AA' is implied by 'A'. For example, the concept 'invoice paid' could imply the concept 'account closed'.

Annotation of Property Relationships

Property relationships involve connecting concepts through *two* one-way relations, each of which can be annotated with the following:

1) The *role* that the target concept plays in that relationship. For example, in a relationship between the concepts 'person' and 'person', one role could be 'child' and the other 'parent', or 'wife' and 'husband' (see Figure 9.12).

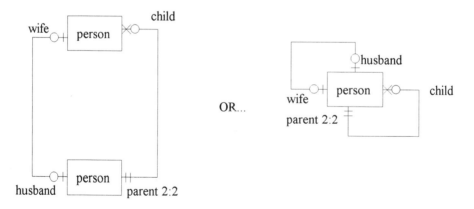

Figure 9.12 Roles, Optionality and Cardinality

2) The *optionality* of the relationship, sometimes referred to as the *lower bound* of the property. This indicates the minimum number of instances of the target which must be present in the relationship. If this minimum number is zero, the relationship is optional, shown as a circle (for '0') located on the link at the target end. For a mandatory property - or a minimum of one or more instances - a bar (for '1') is used. For example, the minimum number of children that a person can have is zero (see Figure 9.12), whereas the minimum number of parents is two. If the exact number of minimum instances is known, this is written after the role as in Figure 9.12.

3) The *cardinality* of the relationship, sometimes referred to as the *upper bound* of the property. This shows the maximum number of instances of the target which may enter in the relationship. If the maximum number is not known in advance, the symbol used is an asterisk located on the link at the target end. For example, one person may be the parent of many children (see Figure 9.12). If the exact number of instances is known, this is written after the role, preceded by a colon: in Figure 9.12 the maximum number of parents is two.

Optionality and cardinality together provide the upper and lower bounds for a property relationship. Four combinations of optionality and cardinality are then possible:

- *zero-to-one* would be appropriate, for example, in both directions of a marriage relationship modelled between the concepts 'man' and 'woman' - any man or woman is either unmarried or married to only one person of the opposite sex; another example could be the relationship between two companies which may or may not be clients of each other;

- *zero-to-many* would model the motherhood relationship from concept 'woman' to concept 'child' — any instance of 'woman' may have zero or more children; another example could be the orders placed by a company on another;

- *one-to-one* would model the motherhood relationship from concept 'child' to concept 'woman' — any instance of 'child' must have one, and only one, mother; another example could apply to an employee who is employed by only one company;

- *one-to-many* would model the relationship from concept 'client' to concept 'account' — a client is assumed not to be a client unless an account has been opened, but any number of additional accounts may be opened subsequently by the same client.

In this discussion we have interpreted a single bar across a link as indicating a cardinality of 'one'. In fact, the single bar can be used to indicate that any fixed, non-zero number of target entities are related to a source entity. For example, in a parenthood relationship between 'child' and 'adult' concepts, every child must have precisely two parents.

By convention, we always group together the annotations — role, optionality and cardinality — at the target end of the link. So, in Figure 9.12 for instance, we read the diagram as follows: a person must have exactly two 'persons' as parents; a person may have several children and a person may have another person as a wife or as a husband.

METAMODELS

As an illustration of the use of concept diagrams, we can express the concepts in Value Analysis as the diagram shown on Figure 9.13. This is an example of a 'metamodel' or a model of the model.

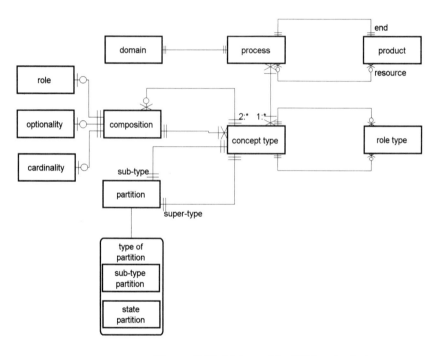

Figure 9.13 Metamodel of Value Analysis

Any other method or technique can be expressed in this way.

STEPS OF CONCEPT MODELLING

If only concept modelling is performed, in isolation from value analysis or event modelling, the following steps are recommended:

1) *identify the domain*: if no process architecture is available, then define as precisely as possible the viewpoint of the analysis; for a process, define the purpose or end result of the process;

2) *identify the main concepts in the domain as a result of discussion*: the end result or the critical objects;

3) *identify the relationships between the concepts*: properties or composition, sub-types and super-types;

4) *identify and record the states of the concepts*;

5) *question whether the 'right level of abstraction has been modelled*: some concepts cannot be described by a 'super-type' if their sub-types are not really states;

6) *repeat steps 2 to 6 until the diagram is*:

- clear — even elegant — and simple: a complicated diagram is the sign that the analysis cannot be left in that state,

- precise and unambiguous,

- complete or consistent in the perspective which has been adopted.

SUMMARY

The technique and notations that we have seen in this chapter have all the necessary and sufficient requirements for modelling concepts in business processes and systems. In practice any notions in other fields can be modelled in this way. They can be used for modelling business situations as well as technical design problems. Although very precise and formal, the diagrams can be understood by a wide range of participants in the process design, including managers, users and designers.

In the next chapter we shall address the dynamics of a situation and how the processes affect the states of the concepts, giving us a complete picture of reality.

Chapter 10

Event Modelling

INTRODUCTION

The static analysis of the concepts relevant to a logical process is carried out in the concept modelling activity discussed in the previous chapter. The dynamics of the concepts will be captured as a sequence of events. In the event model we capture the behaviour of the process where concepts change state. We shall define the preconditions, the activities and the post-conditions (the results) of a process. This is arguably the most difficult activity discussed in this book — but the rewards in terms of quality of results will be worth the effort. Event modelling is also the best foundation for the definition of automated information or workflow automation systems.

EVENTS

An event is defined formally as '*the occurrence or the termination of an instance of a concept*', in other words, the creation or deletion of an actual entity. For example, when a process has completed the validation of the particular invoice number 4321, we could say that we have the event 'validated invoice numbered 4321'. This is an instance of the general event 'validated invoice'.

More generally, an event is the change in state of a concept which may be:

- the *creation* of an instance;

- the *termination* of an instance;

- the *reclassification* of an instance (in effect, the combination of a termination of an entity in one state and its creation in another state).

For example, an invoice might be 'raised', 'due', 'overdue', 'paid', 'archived' (see Figure 10.1).

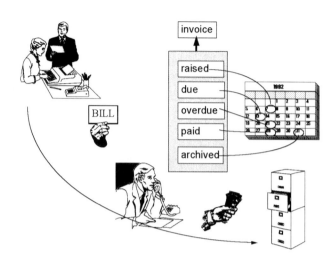

Figure 10.1 The States of an Invoice

In our discussion, the *occurrence* of an event *is the change of state*. It does not have any duration and it is not the steady state of the concept. In common parlance, an event could be a sport event of a musical event which would last for some time. In process modelling, the term *episode* is preferable.

Once it has occurred, an event cannot be undone. The fact that an invoice is paid does not remove the fact that there was at some time in the past a 'due invoice'. It is usual practice for computer program designers to 'delete' records when their processing is complete. In most real business situations, however, this is nonsensical as the notion of deleting an event cannot be entertained (see Figure 10.2). What can be deleted is the *record* of the event (unfortunately in many cases). In situations when an audit trail is mandatory (e.g. in pharmaceutical or defence industries), this consideration is quite natural. Conceptually, every occurrence of an event (every instance of an event) is recorded in the big computer in the sky with a stamp of its date and time of the occurrence.

Figure 10.2 The Occurrence of an Event is Time Stamped

Deleting the record in our earthly computers should be the exception dictated by the implementation constraints of data storage, rather than the norm. When designing processes we should assume that events exist for ever — until we reach the implementation stage. The technical term for this property is *persistence*. New database architectures have had to be developed to support efficiently the persistence of business data (Ling and Bell 1992).

Event diagrams document our understanding of the event sequences. We shall draw as many event diagrams as we need. Since a concept may exist in a number of states, there may be more than one diagram for any one concept. A diagram, however, is not restricted to modelling only one concept state change; a number of concepts may appear in a given diagram.

In process modelling we shall only concern ourselves with types of events. But for convenience, and when there is no ambiguity possible, we shall use the term event to designate an 'event type' and 'event diagram' to mean 'event type diagram'.

Event Modelling

An event is 'the creation, the termination or change of state of a concept' but we have to remember that this is the result of a process. In the model, we should therefore really show the process and its end result — the event (see Figure 10.3). A process is triggered when some preconditions are satisfied. But, as we are mainly concerned with showing the sequence of events, we can use a short-hand notation where the process is 'hidden' behind the event symbol.

The notation for an event is a simple rectangular node with its name inside, which also represents the process which produces it. The event is a place holder for the process. In this chapter we shall often refer to the event to mean the process and its end-event.

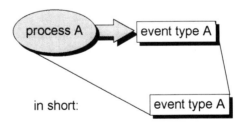

Figure 10.3 A Processor and its End-Event

The link with the Value-Added model can now be seen more clearly. The process architecture introduced in Value Analysis modelling is consistent with this more precise and formal description of the process and its end-product discussed in this chapter. But in this event model, we are also introducing the notion of creation — or termination — of the instances of the end-product. All these apparently different models are in fact different views of the same reality — a business or system.

Sub-Types of Events

Events may be sub-typed using a similar notation to the state sub-typing of concept types in the concept model but obviously only state partitions are allowed. Consistent with the rules of partitioning, the sub-types of events are also mutually exclusive and several partitions can be applied to the same event as illustrated in Figure 10.4.

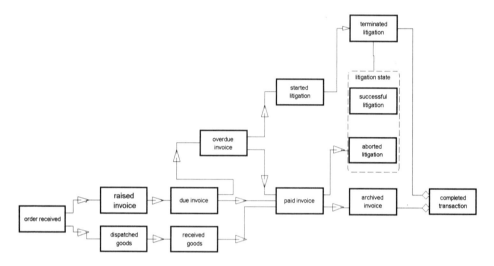

Figure 10.4 The Life of an Invoice

The diagram shows the different states of an invoice from the point of view of a sales department, displayed as part of the complete processing of an order.

When the list of event sub-types in a partition is exhaustive, the partition is referred to as being a 'closed set'. Any instance of the event will be of one and only one sub-type of that event. If all possible sub-types are not exhaustively listed, this is indicated by an empty node in the list meaning 'all other sub-types of this event' which creates an open-set portion. An event may itself be an event sub-type.

TRIGGERING

The preconditions for an event are described with its triggering model (see Figure 10.5).

A number of triggers can be applied to an event. They indicate that the process responsible for the event can be started when the existence of a specific state of some other concept has been satisfied. The event does not have to occur immediately, but it could happen at some unspecified time when the process completes its task.

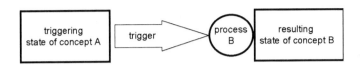

Figure 10.5 Elements of Event Modelling

Types of Triggers

There are two types of triggering situations: unconditional and conditional.

A simple unconditional trigger is when the occurrence of event A is enough to trigger event B. Instead of just one event, there could also be several independent unconditional triggers. A conditional trigger is when several triggers must exist for the trigger to occur (see Figure 10.6).

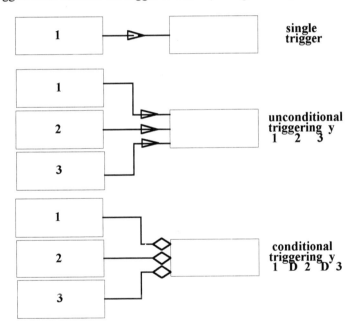

Figure 10.6 Triggering Modes

For example, if events E1, E2 and E3 in Figure 10.6 are the end-events of three streams, we may have the following situations (using logical ORs and ANDs):

1) event E may be triggered by E1 OR E2 OR E3; or

2)   event E cannot be triggered until E1 AND E2 AND E3 have occurred.

In order to model the 'AND' case, we shall use the *'composition'* trigger, similar to the composition used in concept modelling because the composed event E is 'made of' events E1, E2 and E3. A single composition trigger indicates an implication: the source event implies the target event; 'paid order', say, might imply 'completed order'.

Any combination of triggers can be constructed with these elementary AND and OR triggers. For example, Figure 10.7 shows the diagram for the requirement: 'the invoice is cleared if [the value is less than £100] OR [if the customer is not new AND the value is less than £1000] OR [it has been cleared by the Supervisor]'.

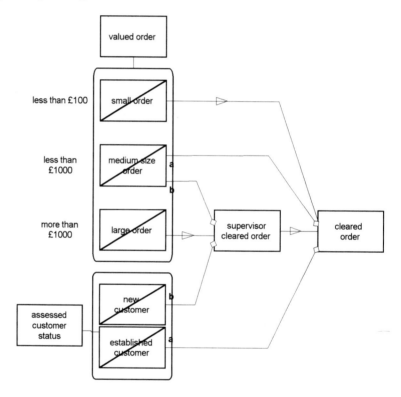

Figure 10.7 Logical Combination of Triggers

Parallel Streams and Synchronisation

Parallel processing streams can be brought together in two ways: synchronised or not. If the two streams can trigger independently the joining event (simple or 'OR' trigger) then there is no synchronisation. In the case of an 'AND' trigger then all the converging streams must wait until all of them are ready.

Recursive Triggers

Although a rare occurrence, the enabling of an event by the occurrence of an event of the same type may also be modelled. Such a *recursive trigger* can be a conditional trigger.

Batches of Triggers

Triggers may be annotated to indicate cardinality, referred to in this context as the *batching of triggers* (see Figure 10.8). The default is when each occurrence of the source event A triggers event B.

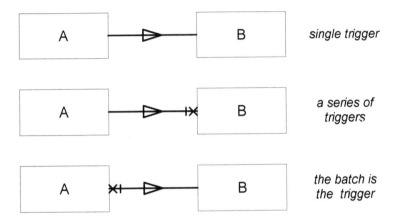

Figure 10.8 Batches of Triggers

However, the diagram shows we may have to wait for the availability of a batch of events A before B is triggered, as would be the case when processing an order where all the lines of the order must be treated before the order can be declared treated. This is *triggering by a batch*.

The last case of interest is when a series of triggers results from a single event, for example opening an order may trigger a number of order line treatments. More formally, any of the following situations can be represented:

1) *one-to-one*: the default situation, one trigger from A causes a single event of type B;

2) *one-to-many*: a single trigger from A may cause a number of target events of type B;

3) *many-to one*: a number of triggers from A are needed to cause a single event of type B;

4) *many-to-many*: the rare occurrence when a series of batches of event A are expected to trigger B or, in other words, an unspecified number of triggers

from A cause another unspecified number of events of type B — this usually indicates further analysis is required to resolve a confusing situation.

What we cannot express with the current notation for a composite trigger is the case where all the triggering events must occur simultaneously. The only condition that we consider is that all the events must have occurred at some time in the past and the last one in the set produces the triggering.

ACTION AND DECISION EVENTS

Events exist in two forms:

1) *Action Event*: the underlying process always results in that event; for example, a 'test' always results in a 'tested part'.

2) *Decision Event*: the underlying process evaluates at least one condition and, depending on the result of the evaluation, either an event takes place or the processing terminates with no outcome. We have then a 'decision event'. The possible outcome of a decision event is 'event' or 'no event' when the process terminates without outcome. We indicate this on the event diagram by a diagonal line across the event node (see Figure 10.9). For example, of the two events 'valid order' and 'non-valid order', only one of them would terminate with an outcome.

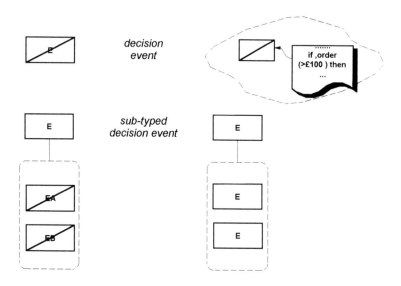

Figure 10.9 Decision Events

If the event is an action and not a decision, at least one and only one of its sub-types must occur, because the partition is an exhaustive and exclusive list.

Processors

The details of the working of the process behind the event are hidden but can also be described by an event diagram. The level of detail which is sufficient for the implementation of the process is reached when only indivisible processes appear on the model and we can consider these processes as 'black boxes'. These indivisible 'atomic' processes are formally known as *elementary processes* or *processors*, and the related events as *elementary events* (see Figure 10.10).

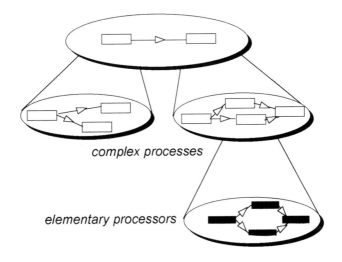

Figure 10.10 Levelling of Events

An elementary event from one point of view can be a complex event from another one. For example, if a travel agent needs the event 'checked seat availability' and is not concerned how this is achieved, then this is an elementary event for that process. But it is a different story on the airline, for whom 'checked seat availability' is rather complex.

The actual implementation of a processor depends on the perspective and can take the form of a procedure for a human actor, a single machine operation or an IT application.

An OO approach is especially suited for implementing the processors identified in the logical model. The notions of pre- and post-conditions, state transitions and encapsulation of the script (the 'method' in OO terms) are completely consistent with a subsequent OO development which could exploit the candidate business objects defined in the model (Meyer 1992 and Martin and Odell 1992).

End Event and Side Effect

An event diagram generally takes the shape of a diamond, indicating that most of the routes to the single end event can be reached from the single start event. The direction of triggers is, overall, from left to right.

Most frequently, a diagram is built from the end event backwards (i.e. right to left), until a start event is identified. The identity of the start event is not always known when the modelling activity is started, whereas in other cases both start and end events are known. In the example of the barber shop, the start event is 'opened shop' and the end event is 'closed shop'.

If we find that we end up with more than one end event, this is an indication that the model is not consistent or is not at a sufficient level of abstraction. We must then analyse the 'end game' and to try to identify a super event which integrates all the separate end events. For example, 'rejected order' and 'accepted order' should be treated as sub-types of the event 'processed order' (see Figure 10.11).

In some cases there are 'side effects' which are modelled as separate end-events. For example, 'identified fraud' could be a side-effect alongside 'processed order' (see Figure 10.11).

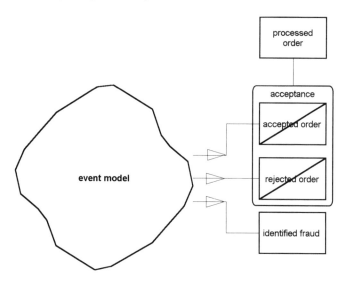

Figure 10.11 Side Effect and Complex End Event

Critical Events

Any event related to the concept(s) in the end result of a process is critical and in particular the event describing the change of state into the end result of the process is the most critical event in that process. For example, in the case of the validation of an order, the chain of events from 'received order' leading to 'validated order' is the critical chain. At a more global level, if the end-product of a customer service is a 'satisfied customer', any event which contributes to the concept 'satisfied customer' is critical for that process. This not only includes the actual deliverable but also its assessment and reporting.

NAMING OF EVENTS

Since an event is the result of the action of a processor, the same name should be given to the event and the processor — a name which expresses the occurrence of an event, such as 'rejected order' or 'available product', in preference to 'order rejected' or 'product available' or, even worse, 'product'.

If we are using design tools to create our model, we may find that some tools demand that we must separate the words in the name by something other than a space, for example by using underscore characters (as in 'validated_order') or by capitalisation (as in 'Validated Order').

EXAMPLE OF AN EVENT MODEL

For example, an event diagram for a 'barber shop' process is shown on Figure 10.12. The situation modelled might be described as follows by the shop owner:

'The shop has two barbers, each of whom is given a chair to cut customer's hair. There are four chairs available for customers to sit in while they wait. Moreover, the shop has a cashier who works at a desk and a magazine rack with magazines for use by customers. If a barber is free when a customer walks in, the customer sits in the barber's chair and has his hair cut. Otherwise, the customer has to wait until the barber is free. While waiting, the customer takes a magazine from the rack and reads it. However, if no barber is free and all the waiting chairs are occupied, the customer gives a "disappointed look" and leaves. A customer whose hair cut is complete will examine the cut, pay the cashier and leave the shop. If the customer is disappointed with the cut he will "give a disappointed look" before leaving.' (IDEF 1992).

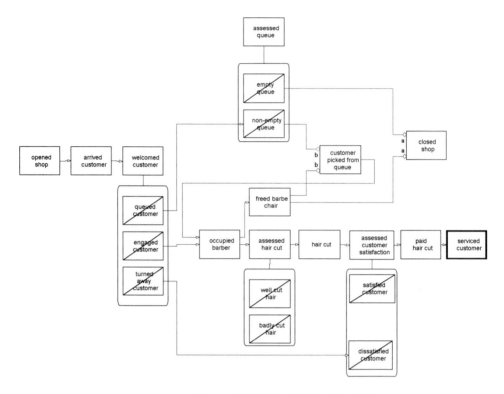

Figure 10.12 The 'Barber Shop' Process

This example is for a particular type of shop. However, by replacing the process it also becomes applicable to a wide range of other situations. For example, the same generic model could be used for the processing of customers in a bank, or on a shop floor or in the processing of a stream of parts by a batch of machines. This shows that the effort put in seeking the abstract concepts and events in a given situation can produce generic models which can be reused.

The model combines a 'flow diagram' with a 'state transition diagram' showing the transformations of a given concept or object. Equipped with this model, we can answer questions such as: Under which conditions is the barber busy? When is a customer dissatisfied? What is the role of the queue? When can the shop be closed? What are the possible states of 'hair'? If we had drawn a flow diagram instead, it would be difficult to answer some of these questions.

Decision Diagrams and Flow Diagrams

Event diagrams are not decision or flow diagrams. Flow diagrams are easy to draw and usually describe the perceived reality of a process. They can be easily converted to code for programming. But they are difficult to abstract and turn into a generic model, not easy to maintain and not very resilient to changes in circumstances. We can avoid these difficulties if we perform concept and event modelling together. Event modelling is a form of state transition model but with the benefit of sub-typing of events. Event modelling can replace techniques such as Entity Life History in SSADM, Petri Nets, the Statechart or the Ward-Mellor STD state transition techniques (Davis 1988).

A number of events connected in series by triggers shows a sequential processing stream. However, this *does not indicate a flow of entities*, but a sequence of change of states.

METAMODEL

We can use a concept diagram to describe the event model as shown in Figure 10.13.

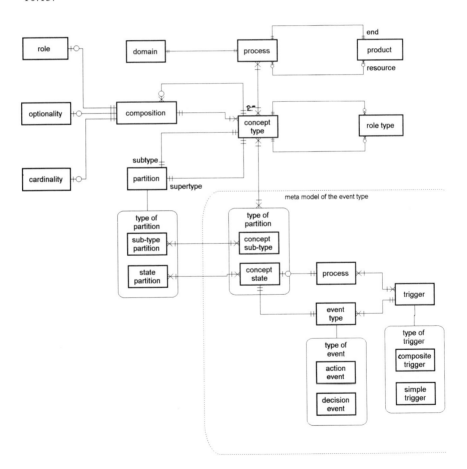

Figure 10.13 Metamodel of Event Modelling

The box 'process' appears twice in the diagram but refers to the same concept. In one case it represents the process introduced in Value-Added modelling and the second case, the process which is responsible for the change of state of a concept — an event in event modelling. There is no real difference in nature between the two interpretations but there is a difference of context, detail and precision. At the most detailed level, a process will be an elementary process or processor.

STEPS IN EVENT MODELLING

If the modelling of event is performed on its own, the following steps are recommended:

1) identify the domain and the end event ('cutting hair' or 'life of the barber shop'?);

2) for each event, starting with the end event, generalise the event ('hair cut' or 'transaction finished'?);

3) identify the events: creation, termination, classification, declassification (and in particular find out what is the *real* underlying type: 'hair cut' or 'satisfied customer'?);

4) define the processor (action or decision) and the triggering conditions, identify the triggering events;

5) determine the sub-types and super-types ('order processed' as a super-type of 'order rejected' and 'order accepted');

6) rename and combine duplicate events and implied events;

7) repeat steps 2) to 6) until each event is completely understood, beginning with a single start event;

8) verify the existence of side-effect event;

9) refine and evaluate the results for completeness, appropriate level of details (too much detail?), level of complexity (too complex?), representativity (does it 'feel right'?);

10) if required, document each event with the script of the associated processor.

SUMMARY

Event modelling supports the dynamic analysis of logical processes. The model is a state transition model. The steady state of the concept is not considered. The process associated with an event can be an action or a decision.

The model is documented with event diagrams. The details of the working of the process are hidden but can also be described by an event diagram. The level of detail which is sufficient for the implementation of the process is reached when only indivisible, elementary processes appear on the model.

The event modelling can answer the following questions:

- What state a concept (an object) can be in?

- What state transition can occur?

- What events can occur?

- What process can take place in a given state?

- What are the operations executed when a process is triggered?

- What is the script (the method in Object-Oriented terms) executed to effect the transition between one state and another?

- What trigger rules apply?

- What is the protocol of the interaction between objects (i.e. content of the message passing)?

In the next chapter, we shall see how the three modelling techniques — Value-Added, Concept and Event modellings - come together in order to create the logical model of the processes.

Chapter 11

Steps in Value Analysis

INTRODUCTION

A value analysis of a process is expressed through the three views:

- *value-added modelling*: giving the overall architecture of the processes,
- *concept modelling*: giving a static view of the processes,
- *event modelling*: extending the model with a dynamic analysis of the events taking place within the processes.

From these views, we can identify the critical concepts, events and processes. These steps should not be followed in a strict 'water-fall' type linear progression from value-added modelling through concept modelling to event modelling. In fact, the modelling activity is far more one of iteration and re-work.

Modelling in the value-added model does not need to be complete before progressing to concept and event modelling. The three techniques proceed in parallel as complementary activities. Extension and refinement of the model of one technique may require rework in either of the other two techniques.

In this chapter we shall look more closely at the method — the steps — for the whole value modelling. The overall method is summarised as a process in the diagram shown on Figure 11.1.

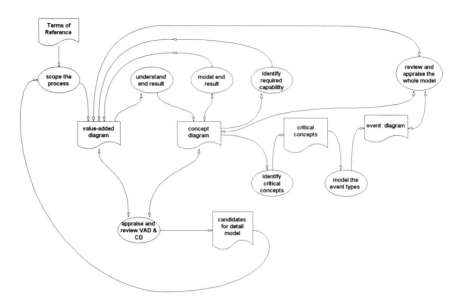

Figure 11.1 Overall Method for Value Analysis

There are eight main activities in the process and these are detailed in the next sections.

Step 1. Scope the Process

The scope represents the domain of a process. It is not critical to be precise at this stage — the precision will come later from a better understanding of the model, when the boundary will be clearer.

Step 2. Understand the End Result

This is the most difficult and the most important activity of the modelling. We must understand the end result of the process before we can proceed further: the end results can be expressed as the mission or the goal or the deliverables. A concept diagram is used to document it. The end-result must have a value that is potentially quantifiable — it is always a capability for someone else.

Step 3. Model End Result

The concepts in the end result must be challenged and refined by asking questions like:

- Is it at the right level of abstraction?

- Is it too general?

- Is it too specific?

- Is it a measurement of something else?

The definition of all concepts should be agreed and recorded in a concept diagram.

Step 4. Identify the Required Capabilities

The candidate capabilities from the concept diagram need to be identified: the components of the concepts defining the end result. The output from this phrase is a value-added model which starts by drawing up a first-cut value-added diagram (VAD). Only the end result and required capabilities are important — not the name.

Step 5. Appraise the Value-Added and Concept Models

The aim should be to create simple or even elegant diagrams, displayng symmetry and clusters of nodes which are easy to understand. Even with limited experience, it is easy to develop a feeling for the soundness of a diagram from its visible appearance, for instance by looking out for:

- relationships and concepts which belong to another level of detail;

- real or apparent end results and capabilities;

- duplication or restrictive definition (need for more abstraction).

Step 6. Identify Critical Concepts and Events

The critical concepts are those which are:

- part of the end result, especially those concepts which have states critical to the end-result,

- critical in the eyes of the business players.

Candidate concepts become end results and capabilities within a more detailed level of modelling. Produce:

- Value-added diagrams (VAD) expanded onto decomposed value-added diagram;

- Concepts in decomposed value-added diagrams analysed in further concept diagrams.

Repeat steps 1 to 6 until the desired level of detail is achieved.

Step 7. Model the Event Types

An event diagram models the change in state of concepts. The events may have previously appeared as states in a concept state partition of a concept diagram. The critical concepts identified in the previous steps are those which are modelled first, through the following:

1) Identify the domain and the end event ('cutting hair' or 'life of the barber shop'?);

2) For each event, starting with the end event, generalise the event ('hair cut' or 'transaction finished'?) using approaches such as:

- *creation*: e.g. 'created', 'started', 'identified', 'defined', 'effected';

- *termination*: e.g. 'closed', 'finished', 'completed', 'removed', 'archived';

- *classification*: e.g. 'account overdrawn'.

   Identified events may require sub-typing to record the existence of sub-types relevant to the domain under study. Conversely, some events may be identified as being sub-types of some higher abstraction, a 'super-type' event.

3) Define the processor (action or decision) and the triggering conditions. If required, document each event with a script of the associated processor.

4) Identify the triggering events. Determine the triggering events - build up a network of triggers which 'fans out' from the endevent, by asking questions such as: Which other event must occur before this one? OR which others? AND which others?

5) Determine the sub-types and super-types (e.g. 'order processed' as a super-type of 'order rejected' and 'order accepted').

6) Rename and combine duplicate events and implied events. You may discover that the same event has appeared in two or more places, but has been given a different name in each case. These may be reconciled to simplify the model. Where an implication link has been used in the model, this situation should be examined to determine if the concepts it connects are truly separate types or may be joined as a single event.

7) Repeat 2) to 6) until each critical event is completely understood ending with a single start event. The process of identifying all events which can trigger the end event is repeated for each of the new events. This continues repeatedly along every branch of the developing network of event and triggers, until the start-event for the event diagram is found.

8) Verify the existence of any side effect event that may have been identified. These should be challenged to determine whether they are true side effects or, for example, may just be sub-types of some other event of the model.

9) Refine and evaluate the results for completeness and appropriate levels of detail (too much detail?), complexity (too complex?) and representativity (does it 'feel right'?).

Step 8 Review and Appraise the Whole Model

Review the value-added and concept models with the deeper understanding acquired while creating the event model.

SUMMARY

The deliverables from the value analysis modelling include the following:

- Value-added diagram (VAD) and decomposed value-added diagrams: documenting the architecture of the logical processes;

- Concept diagrams (CD): identification of the concepts, their states possible, their meaning and their relationships;

- Event diagram (ED): the model of the concept states identified in concept diagrams and, optionally, the textual or diagrammatic script documenting the processors behind the events.

This model gives us the elements with which we are going to construct the implementable processes which take account of the options and preferences of the organisation.

Part IV
Implementation of Physical Processes

Chapter 12

Designing the Physical Processes

INTRODUCTION

This chapter addresses the physical set-up of the activities in the organisation, bringing together the 'vertical' organisational view and the 'horizontal' logical view.

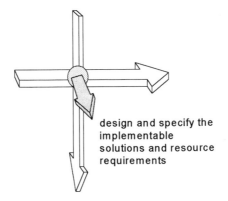

design and specify the implementable solutions and resource requirements

Figure 12.1 The 'Diagonal' Physical View

If the process in steps suggested in Chapter 5 Process Improvement Projects are followed, the following should have been established:

- a documented understanding of the mission, goals and objectives;

- a value model of the required logical processes;

- the prioritised issues relevant to the area under study;

- the existing or proposed organisation — quantified with the business constraints such as: types of business units; geographical hierarchy;

organisational hierarchy; security hierarchy; and market sector size and requirements.

We now have all the elements to tackle the design of the actual physical processes from which we will specify the resources that we need.

IMPLEMENTABLE AND PHYSICAL PROCESSES

At this point, the temptation is to dive directly into designing the activities for each type of business unit at each location: for example, the new account procedure and systems for 'insurance','loans' and 'investors'. However, there is an advantage in deferring the commitment of physical resources as late as possible. This will give the additional flexibility to adapt to local situations.

We shall then proceed in two steps:

1) designing the *implementable processes*: defining generic activities, as a grouping of logical processes, using the notation of process mapping;

2) specifying the *physical processes* 'in-situ' in each required location; using full textual descriptions, supported by an enhancement of the process mapping notation showing the physical attributes.

Implementable Processes

The abstract Value Analysis model has provided us with the business events. We can now group the events into clusters within which there is a higher degree of interaction (information or material). We shall also take into account the constraints of the organisation in terms of geography (existing business units or physical constraints) and reporting structure (existing divisions or cultural boundaries which need to be preserved, at least for the time being). The result is a set of convenient operational 'functions' of closely related activities which can be managed by a single team. The events in the value analysis gives us the elementary building blocks of the activities, and their triggering conditions give us the interface between activities, the protocol of the interactions.

We shall call these groupings of activities *implementable processes*, which are sometimes also called 'business systems' by IT-oriented designers. Examples of implementable processes would be 'order processing', 'customer facing', 'performance monitoring', 'intelligence management'. The culture, practice or tradition in the organisation play a part in deciding this grouping of events. For example, one organisation might have a single 'training', whereas another will split training into 'developing or procuring training courses' and 'delivering training' (see Figure 12.2).

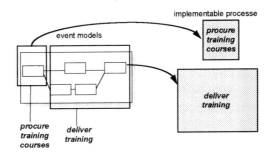

Figure 12.2 Example of Implementable Processes for Training

Physical Process in a Business Unit

Having defined the 'implementable processes', we can then consider each physical location or business unit and specify what is actually required. In a large international group, say, we may have only one 'training development centre' and a 'training delivery unit' in each country, with different language constraints (see Figure 12.3). The specification of the actual people, systems, location and other resources needed for these activities might end up looking very differently at different places in the organisation.

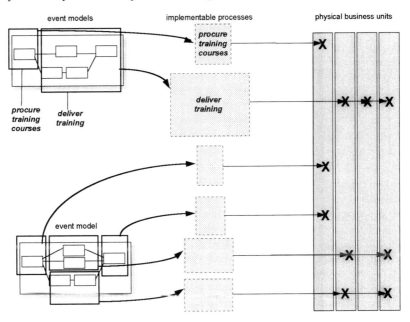

Figure 12.3 Mapping from Events to Implementable Process to Physical Business Units

There is not usually a direct correspondence between a logical process and the visible, physical process at a given location of the organisation. For example, the logical — abstract — process 'opening an account' might be combined with 'checking catalogue of existing products' and 'receiving an order' into a complete customer-facing transaction (see Figure 12.4). This complete transaction could be considered as a package of activities for which we can define the capabilities that it delivers, such as: the quality measurements of its capabilities; the capability that it must have; and the generic roles — the team responsible for it. This will be the description of a generic, implementable process.

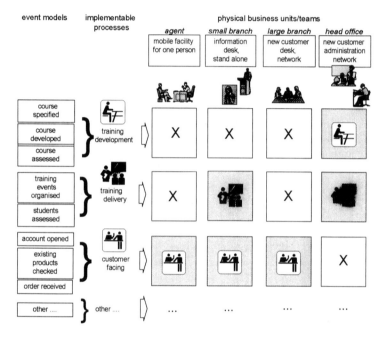

Figure 12.4 Example of Business Units

Concept Model of Improvement Projects

The more technically minded readers might be interested in looking at a concept diagram describing, in a compact form, the notions behind the design and specification of physical processes. Such a *metamodel* is shown in Figure 12.5. (As usual in concept modelling, we use the singular on the diagram in order to emphasise that we are dealing with 'types' of things and not instances: a 'solution type' and not specific 'solutions'.)

We see from this diagram that the *capabilities* — current or required — are imposed by the tactical plan and are the responsibility of a *capability management process*. This defines the *implementable processes* (generic) and will manage the *physical processes*, which embody the implementable processes and should include the expression of *organisation constraints* (the current or future organisation of the business units, geography and people), *business constraints* (market, volume and timing) and identified *issues.*

The gap between the current and required capabilities is expressed as *process requirement(s).* These requirements will be satisfied by *solution(s)* (through the *contribution* of the solutions). These solutions are delivered by projects (improvement or implementation projects). These solutions result in the physical processes. The solutions will always include the already mentioned three aspects: *activities, people* and *logistical means* (e.g. IT systems, communication systems, transport, warehousing). *Enactment, assignment* and *commissioning* are the specific forms of deployment for defined *procedures, trained people* and the other *available resources.*

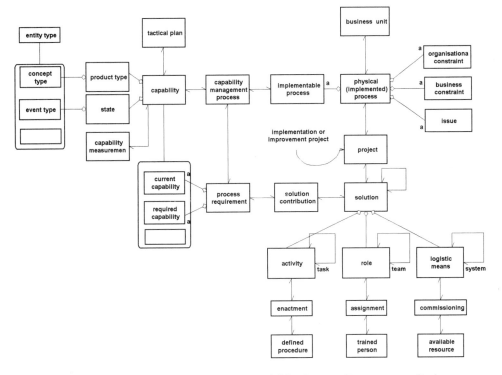

Figure 12.5 Concept Model for Process Improvement Projects

PROCESS DOCUMENTATION

There is a wide choice of techniques and notations for capturing and designing physical processes. We shall review some of the more popular ones in the following sections. Whatever techniques are chosen, we need to be able to document the following:

Implementable processes:

1) *the activities* (also called tasks) which process information or material;

2) *the grouping of activities* into physical processes;

3) *the purpose* of the physical process (expressed as the capabilities which are delivered to the organisation);

4) *the quality measurements* (how we measure the achievement of the purpose);

5) *the capabilities that the process must get* from other implementable processes;

6) the capabilities that the process must have;

7) the *specification of the type of resources needed in the capabilities* in terms of procedures, people and logistical means.

Physical processes (additionally):

8) *the location*: actual site or unit;

9) *the assignment* of activities and processes to individuals and teams;

10) *the logistical means*: IT systems, databases, communication systems, transport, warehousing and other logistical means;

11) *the nature of the information processing*: creating, using or modifying;

12) the flows of information and material;

13) *the measurable attributes* of the activities, which are usually one or several of the following categories:

- human resources — competency, time available, time required per activity,

- material requirement — volume or cost for one activity, for a batch,

- logistical requirements — type, time available, time required for one activity, cost active, cost idle,

- cycle time — the time to complete one activity,

- set-up time — the lead time between batches of identical activities,

- batch size — number of identical activities which can be performed without change of procedure or means.

We will need both textual and diagrammatic documents. All this documentation is necessary for the developers and suppliers of the actual people and logistical systems.

In the following, we shall look at process mapping, team architecture and resource specifications.

PROCESS MAPPING

Process mapping is an ambiguous term used by convention to describe the documentation of processes. We shall use it for three different purposes at three different points of the process improvement cycle proposed in Part II:

1) *Documenting existing activities* (step 2.1 'assess existing processes'): captures the activities actually performed and the issues identified by the people in these activities, as a starting point for a redesign and an opportunity for identifying the problems and issues with the current set-up. There is a danger of spending too much time capturing the current activities. A few sessions in facilitated workshops should be enough. The issues are either *direction, process design* or *process implementation* issues. The documentation includes:

- activity flow diagrams;

- organisational structure (including organisation chart);

- issues.

2) *Implementable processes* (steps 5.1 to 5.4 'define implementable processes') depict the activities in the proposed process, such as:

- the new activity flow diagrams;

- the delivered and needed capabilities;

- the new roles and teams;

- the quality measurements.

3) *Physical processes* (step 7.3 'define resources' and step 9 'resource procurement projects') documents the activities at each location and specify the required resources with their relevant attributes, for example:

- the business constraints (location, volume, timing, typical assignments of roles to organisational ranks or responsibilities);

- the specification of the resources for the new processes;

- the roles and assignments to people, their role and competency descriptions;

- the specification of the logistical means (e.g. IT systems).

The diagrams used for the documentation of the implementable and physical processes include the following:

1) *Activity architecture* (the business processes) describing current processes covering:

- generic implementable processes;

- reusable organisational components;

- physical (implemented) processes with the physical attributes: people or ranks, materials, systems;

- numerical attributes (timing, volume, cost);

- detailed procedure scripts;

- an Activity Measurement Matrix, a quality check on the design.

2) *Management architecture* (the management structure).

3) *Team architecture and team responsibility matrix.*

Narrative descriptions should be attached to each of the diagrams. Using suitable design tools would ensure the consistency between diagrams and between diagrams and textual narratives.

The following sections will consider each of these diagrams in turn.

Activity Architecture

In this section and the following sections, the concept of activity is used to designate the tasks which are the elements of a process. A process has a well-defined outcome (delivering a capability), whereas activities may only be described by the actions which are undertaken. The actions can be simple actions — always resulting in the same output — or decisions — resulting in one of several possible outputs.

Activity Flow Diagram

Any convenient notation can be used for activity flow diagrams. An example of the *a*BC*d* notations is shown in Figure 12.6.

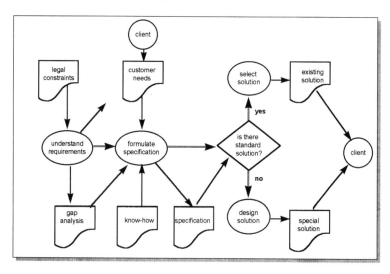

Figure 12.6 Example of Activity Flow Diagram

The symbols on the diagram are defined on Figure 12.7. (The notations used here are from the *a*BC*d*™ method which is derived from the results of this book, the complete set is shown in Chapter 15.)

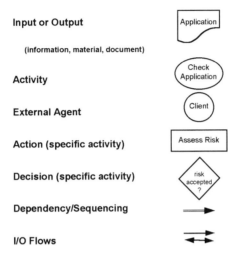

Figure 12.7 *a*BC*d* Notation used for Activity Flow Diagrams

The description of the activities should be completed by a textual description, including:

- a short name (a convenient label or number);

- a longer, more meaningful name explaining the purpose (WHAT is the activity for?);

- the capabilities that it needs (WITH what?) in terms of procedures, people and other resources;

- the applicable approach or policies (HOW?);

- the quality measurements; and the physical attributes (when, where, how often, how fast, how costly) in the case of a physical process or activity.

Decomposed Activity Flow Diagram

A process can be documented at a higher level of detail with a Decomposed Activity Flow Diagram. For example, the process of 'order processing' can be decomposed into 'checking order', 'checking catalogue', 'checking stock', 'checking credit', 'issuing store pick list', 'getting from store', 'packing' and 'dispatching'. The decomposition can be repeated, for example for 'checking credit', down to the level where the level of documentation is enough for the purpose of the analysis — usually the tasks of an individual role.

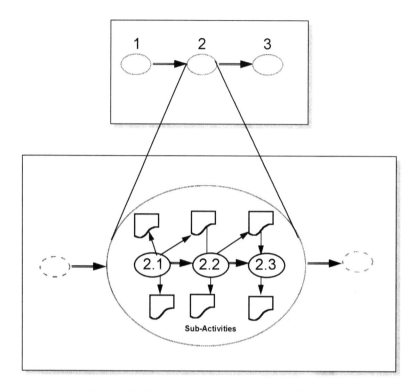

Figure 12.8 Decomposed Activity Flow Diagram

Decisions

Decisions can be shown as a special notation on the *activity flow diagram* (for example, diamond shaped activities as shown on Figure 12.7). An example of *decisions* on an activity flow diagram is shown on Figure 12.9.

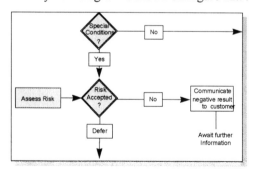

Figure 12.9 Decisions on an Activity Flow Diagram

It is often recommended that decisions should only be shown at the most detailed level — at the 'leaves' of the activity flow diagrams. This is a matter of choice for the design team.

IDEF0

One of the earlier modelling techniques in systems development was Structure Analysis and Design Technique (SADT™). The 'actigram' in SADT is a representation of the activities showing the flow of information and control between them. The actigram is the basis of the widely used IDEF0 notation adopted by the process engineers in some sectors of the manufacturing industry (IDEF 1992). In the European manufacturing industry, a set of generic process models and organisational modelling techniques has been recently derived from IDEF0, under the name CIM-OSA. The convention used for IDEF0 diagrams is shown on Figure 12.10.

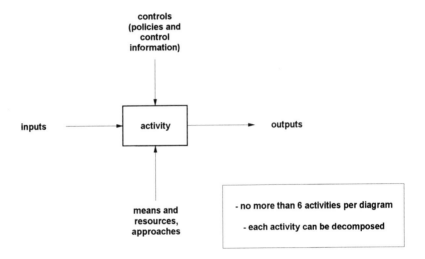

Figure 12.10 IDEF0 Diagrams Conventions

An example of a simple IDEF0 diagram is shown on Figure 12.11.

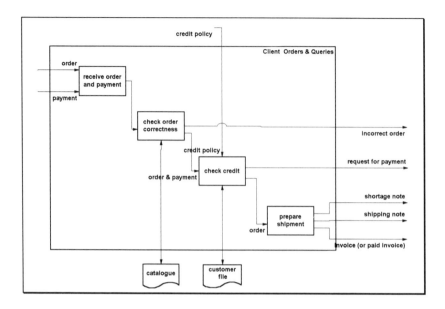

Figure 12.11 Example of IDEF0 Diagram

IDEF0 is an elegant notation for showing activities and processes. However, it has some shortcomings: it lacks the foundation and rationale of process architecture for guiding process engineers in constructing 'good' models and it requires a discipline which is not always suitable for informal process mapping and communication.

Role Activity Diagram (RAD)

For an informal capture of an existing process and for designing new physical processes, the Role Activity Diagram (RAD) is arguably the most natural notation for the operators in the process. It is also a good notation for the programming of many automated workflow systems (Ould 1995).

RAD invites the analyst or designer to see the processes from the point of view of each role in turn. Following different threads of activities, a picture emerges of the set of actions performed by each role and the interaction between them. Figure 12.12 shows an example of RAD. It shows parallel threads, synchronisation and the responsibility for each activity.

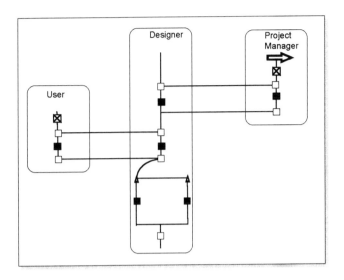

Figure 12.12 Example of a Role Activity Diagram
(reproduced with the kind permission of Praxis plc)

The limitation of RAD is that it can lead to very detailed, low level activity descriptions, which makes it difficult to identify and document the logical or reusable implementable processes.

The summary of the notations on a RAD is shown in Chapter 15.

Capability Measurement, Quality Measurement

The quality of the design is measured by the ability of the activities to deliver the required contribution to the organisation objectives; in order words, the provision of some capability required by the organisation.

We shall capture this with a matrix and/or a diagram showing how many of the proposed activities each contributes to the organisation objectives or capabilities (see Figure 12.13). One matrix and/or diagram should be drawn for each implementable process. The diagram gives a simple visual check of which activity contributes to which objective. The matrix gives the same cross reference but also allows us to write down a subjective estimate of the degree of the contribution. If an objective is completely addressed by one activity, the relevant cell will show 100%. If two activities share this equally, each will receive the value 50%. This is not meant to be an accurate measurement but a subjective check (a 'guestimate').

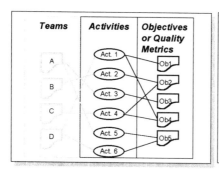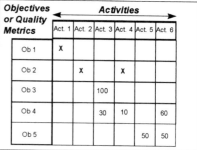

Figure 12.13 Process Quality Diagram and Matrix

A *process quality diagram and matrix,* as shown in Figure 12.13, is useful for an overview of the contribution of each activity and for a check of the adequate cover of each required capability.

TEAM ARCHITECTURE

The definition of the team results from the analysis of the 'people' capabilities required for an implementable process. These considerations are complemented by the need to separate some of the roles: directing, leading and measuring, for example. The notion of separation of powers, which has been the foundation of most democratic societies since the French Revolution, is a good guideline.

Team Architecture Diagram

What roles are included in a given team is shown on a *team architecture diagram* (see Figure 12.14).

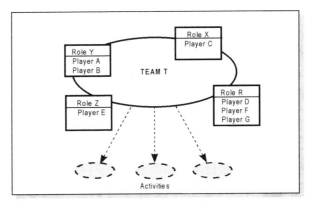

(one team <=> one or several activities)

Figure 12.14 Example of Team Architecture Diagram

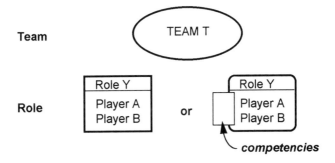

Figure 12.15 Notations on a Team Architecture Diagram

Figure 12.15 shows two alternatives for the notation of roles. It can be either simply a rectangle or an object-oriented type of symbol. In both notations, the role name appears at the top and the name of the role holders appears below — individuals or typical ranks (e.g. police constable, sergeant, superintendent) or recognised functions (e.g. driver, inspector, manager of grade 5).

A diagram is useful to show the relationship between teams, say, using the simple notation in Figure 12.16.

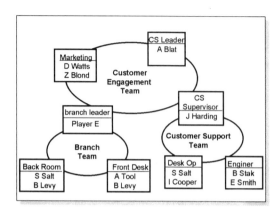

Figure 12.16 Simple Teams Architecture Diagram (Showing a Network of Teams)

Figure 12.17 shows how to represent a 'team of teams' with *a structured team diagram* where we can highlight the competencies required from the team and how they are provided by sub-teams and individuals. This is a team architecture shown with the object-oriented notation of HOOD (Robinson 1992).

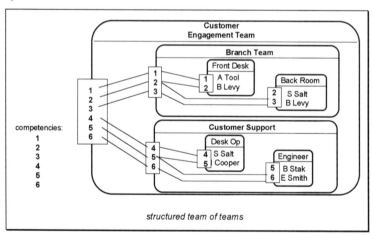

Figure 12.17 Structured Team Diagram

The diagrams should be complemented by a textual description of the roles.

Some of the generic roles often found in process design, together with their contribution are as follows:

- *process leader*: to direct, facilitate and support the process teams, to monitor the quality of the contributions (based on the organisation goals and objectives);

- *process facilitator*: to manage the means, the inputs and the output of the process;

- *process adviser*: to contribute to the process for specific considerations requiring knowledge and understanding not normally expected in the teams;

- *team leader*: to ensure that a team contributes to the agreed goals and objectives, paying attention to the three important team considerations: the task, the group and the individuals;

- *team member*: to play one or several roles in the team and contribute to the achievements of the team. A team member in general relies on the other members to be effective and efficient.

We shall discuss the issue of competency in a later section of this chapter.

Team Role Assignment Diagram and Matrix

A given team may be responsible for several implementable processes. But a given process can only be the responsibility of one team. This is the rule of indivisibility of responsibility.

A matrix or a diagram can be used to show the assignment of teams to processes (see Figure 12.18). A textual description is also usually adequate. On the Team Assignment diagram we can also show the objectives which are pursued in the activities. The quality measurements are always related to these objectives and measurements can be shown instead of the objectives.

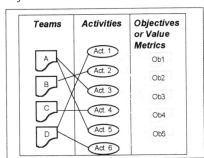

Figure 12.18 Team Assignment Diagram and Matrix

Activities are defined on the basis of their contribution to the overall business objectives. As a result, the activities undertaken by the teams determine directly their objectives and the value measurements of their contribution.

The team assignment diagram (Figure 12.18) and the process quality diagram (Figure 12.13) can be combined.

SUPPORTING SYSTEMS

Systems that describe logistical means are specified and measured in the same manner as the teams: they participate to the logistical means - the third element of the capabilities, in addition to activities, and people. These systems can involve IT, communication, workflow, transport, manufacture and, more generally, any complex logistical means. We can use diagrams similar to team design in order to design and document the architecture of systems.

System Architecture

The object-oriented notation which has served us for showing teams of teams can also be pressed into service for showing the architecture of the logistical means. That notation is convenient in relating the required and provided capabilities with the corresponding logistical means. The example illustrated by Figure 12.19 is part of a set of IT systems and databases that might be required for a project for the support of customer-facing operations in branches of a financial service organisation.

The capabilities shown in Figure 12.19 are:

1) increased customer awareness;

2) understood customer circumstances;

3) evaluated willingness to pay;

4) evaluated security;

5) effective communication with customer;

6) developed customer plan.

The important point to keep in mind is that the specification of the means is a direct result of the needs of the processes, themselves the expression of the capabilities required in the architecture of the implementable processes. Every piece of specification should have a direct relationship with the provision of a capability contributing to the goals and objectives of the organisation. Specifications are expressed in 'business' terms not in technical terms.

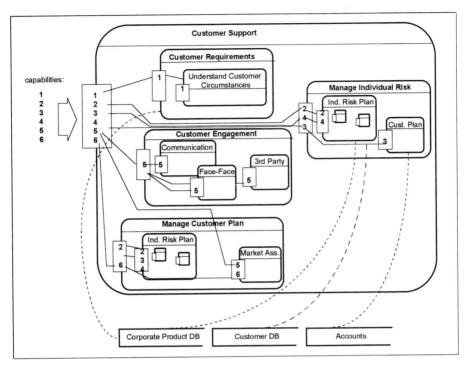

Figure 12.19 Systems Architecture for Branches of a Financial Service

If we have followed the steps and the rationale discussed in the previous chapters, we should be able to make this connection back to the mission, goals and objectives. The 'local' requirements should only be justified by the business constraints of implementing the physical process in that particular locality and no other reasons.

Team Assignment

A matrix or a diagram can be used to show the assignment of systems to processes (see Figure 12.20). A textual description is also usually adequate. On the *system assignment diagram* we can also show the objectives which are pursued in the activities. As for teams, the quality measurements are always related to these objectives and measurements can be shown instead of the objectives.

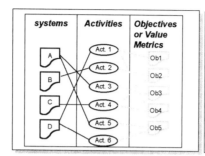
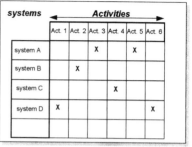

systems	Act. 1	Act. 2	Act. 3	Act. 4	Act. 5	Act. 6
system A			X		X	
system B		X				
system C				X		
system D	X					X

Figure 12.20 System Assignment Diagram and Matrix

The activities supported by the systems determine directly their objectives and the value measurements of their contribution (useful for the specification of the systems!).

RESOURCE SPECIFICATION

The physical implementation of a process requires capabilities made up of three types of resources: activity, people and logistical means (systems). The documentation — preferably written down — of the process capability from the activity point of view takes the form of:

1)   the detailed procedures (activity scripts);

2)   the team and individual role competency description;

3)   the specification of the logistical means: such as IS systems, workflow systems, communication systems, transport means, warehousing, manufacture facilities.

Procedures

The conventions used for writing up the procedures depends on the degree of formality acceptable in each situation. Natural language (e.g. English) can be used, or if the activity is likely to be automated at a latter stage, structured English, a computer language (i.e. Pascal or C++) or even a formal language (i.e. Z or VDM). An object-oriented language like Smalltalk or Eiffel encourages the capture not only of the procedure itself but of its pre- and post-conditions (Meyer 1992). The example shown on Figure 12.21 is written in structured English.

```
Activity Act 4.5 'process order'
      i order received t e
           c ec  stoc
           c ec  credit  ort i ess
           iss e store order
           iss e disp tc  order
           iss e i voice
           pd te c sto er  i e
```

Figure 12.21 Activity Procedure

If scripts were recorded in the logical event model, then the activity procedure is a simple concatenation of the various event scripts.

Competency Description

The issues of the relationship between roles and competency exceed the scope of this book and here we shall only summarise these issues.

The organisation would decide the different categories of competencies which are relevant. The following might be included: understanding or setting direction; customer-facing skills; analytical expertise; team-working skills; and specialised technical know-how. For each category, different levels of achievement would be defined, with appropriate objective tests and training and support means. Each role would then be characterised by a typical profile (see Figure 12.22). The competency scales would also be used by the organisation and the individuals to determine individual profiles. The suitability of an individual for a particular role can be objectively assessed by comparing the two profiles. This would reveal a match, an overqualification or an underqualification. This could be used to determine either the opportunities for moves for taking other roles or for training needs (Spencer and Spencer 1993).

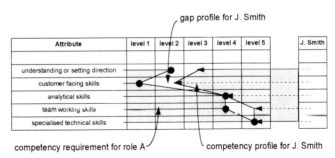

Figure 12.22 Competency Profile

More sophisticated competency profiles could include considerations of skills, behaviour, attitude or other relevant human resource attributes. This approach to human resources has the advantage of relating the individual competencies to the roles that the organisation needs. There should be only one competency grid for the whole organisation at all levels, which should enable individuals to relate to the requirements of roles that they are currently fulfilling or that they wish to fulfil (Tijou 1994).

Specification of the Logistics Means

We shall dedicate the whole of the next chapter to the specification of the logistical means. We note however that the approach that we have followed to design the architecture of the systems shows a direct relationship between the business objectives and the capabilities required from the systems. If an OO method is used for developing the IT systems, we have in hand the business objects with the underlying concepts, their states and their associated scripts (the 'methods' in OO terminology). It is then a natural progression to define the IT objects to be implemented.

EXAMPLE OF AN IMPLEMENTABLE PROCESS

The following shows an example, inspired by an actual case, of the textual description of a CMP for a public service organisation. The role of this CMP is to provide the resources (the material means) needed by the organisation.

CMP Purpose

The formal purpose of this process is:

> 'To make available the servicing resources in the state required for current and future delivery of services.'

The critical capability which is addressed by this process is:

- Committed means of delivery.

CMP Own Capabilities

The capabilities that this process must have are as follows:

- Defined required servicing capability;
- Acknowledged relevant values;
- Planned provision of future servicing capability;
- Managed existing servicing capabilities.

These contribute to the documentation of the tactical plans (e.g. One-Year Business Plans).

CMP Roles

The roles identified in this process are as follows (also shown on a team architecture diagram):

1) **CMP Process Leader:** the role played by the 'Performance Monitor';

2) **CMP Co-ordinator:** the role which organises the working of CMP and administrates the facilities, the logistical means and the material required or produced by the process;

3) **Servicing Adviser:** the role which advises on the extent or limitations of service actions, the options available and the restraints under which the service is provided;

4) **Financial Manager:** the role required to provide a financial perspective in the resource planning;

5) **Resource Procurement Adviser:** the role played by the appropriate 'expert' to advise on how to acquire resources (e.g. financial, human or vehicles) and the way in which to convert them to the required level of readiness in order to deliver the servicing service;

6) **Service Requirements Reporter:** the role which brings to this process the servicing requirements;

7) **CMP Process Evaluator:** the role that monitors the good functioning of this process.

CMP4 Measurements

The measurements are:

- the right capability when needed ('the right person with the right skill, in the right place at the right time');

- the right quality of resource;

- proven operational readiness;

- 'just in time' resources.

The actual instruments to be used to make measurements also need to be defined.

CMP4 Possible New Organisation

The roles identified in the CMP could be related to existing functions as follows (required extensions or new roles are indicated):

CMP4 (Provide Means) roles:	Could equate to:
Managed Existing Servicing Capabilities	VP for Operation
Process Co-ordinator	CMP4 Co-ordinator (to be created)
Servicing Adviser	as required
Financial Manager	Financial Manager
Resource Procurement Adviser	Procurement Manager
Service Requirement Reporter	User Group Representative
Process Evaluator	to be created

Figure 12.23 Possible role assignments for CMP

The detailed assignments should be the subject of more consultations with the Human Resources department.

CMP Meetings

Because this is a management process, meetings between the members of the team are an important part of the process. The minimum set of fixed (regular) CMP meetings is determined by what the process has to deliver. An example of meetings and the roles attending for our example could be as follows (Figure 12.24):

CMP4 (Capability for Servicing) Meetings:	Considerations:
Review of Requirements	Defined Required Servicing Capability
Future Resource Capabilities	Planned Provision of Future Servicing Capability
Existing Resource Management	Managed Existing Servicing Capabilities
Quality and Ethics	Quality Measurements, Acknowledged Relevant Values
Review of the Process	The Design and Implementation of the Process, Review of Issues

Figure 12.24 Possible Fixed Meetings for CMP

CMP Activities

These are also activities between meetings. These activities could be designed according to the generic patterns discussed in Part II and are not repeated here.

SIMULATION OF ACTIVITY FLOWS

The simulation of the proposed physical processes can be tested with a suitable simulation package. Some design tools for activity flow or role activity are capable of using the values of the parameters submitted for different scenarios and to perform simulated runs. For example, an insurance claim processing process can be simulated in order to determine the required number of stations and the likely throughput under different levels of demand.

WORKFLOW DESIGN

There are circumstances which require a high volume of transactions, for example for the processing of insurance claims or regular payments. There are also cases when traceability is one of the critical requirements of the process, for example in the development or manufacture of pharmaceutical products, in financial transaction or in legal transactions. In this case, it is appropriate to consider the automation of the process.

Workflow automation is one of the fastest growing sectors of the IT industry. The techniques outlined in this book for the specification of the implementable process are appropriate in order to front-end the design of such systems. The decision to automate can be left at the last possible opportunity.

CONCLUSIONS

In this chapter we have seen how to integrate the logical model with the constraints of the organisation (geography, reporting structure) and the operational parameters (product and service delivery constraints). The result is a specification for the resources which need to be developed or procured and integrated into improved or new physical processes.

The next chapter addresses the actual formulation of the specifications, in a manner which is consistent with our concern with the delivery of the resources actually required by the organisation. It addresses the selection of the solutions made available by the providers in response to the specifications of these resources.

Chapter 13

Specifying and Planning the Required Resources

INTRODUCTION

The traditional way to specify the required physical resources is either to prepare a detailed requirement document or to leave the providers to ask questions, in the hope that they will be the right questions. The specification is notoriously difficult to write. The result is often long and technically detailed documents in which business managers and operatives have difficulty to recognise the solution to their original needs. This is a frequent cause of misunderstanding and frustration between business and development sides of what should be a co-operative effort.

The largest item of the budget of an organisation is usually its running cost: the salaries, the materials and the maintenance of the plants. The second largest in size is often the capital investment required for setting up the processes and acquiring the required resources. But whereas the running cost is regular and spread over the life of the organisation, the setting-up expenditure is concentrated on a relatively short time (a few months or a few years). The task of specifying the processes and the required resources is very critical and mistakes made at this stage can be the most expensive on the long term. If it turns out that the specified systems and logistical means do not fit their purpose, the costs can be crippling in terms of money or reputation and can even threaten the very existence of the organisation.

There is a better way. Some of the techniques used in process design can be used to facilitate the common understanding of the context, the reasons, the requirements for logistics systems and, in particular, IT systems and applications. The implementation details will be provided later on by the implementors and suppliers. The specification should concentrate on those parameters which are necessary from the 'business' point of view and the users' point of view, on the critical capabilities and their attributes.

The technique described in this chapter follows closely the 'Design by Objective' philosophy developed and promoted by Tom Gilb since the early 1980s (Gilb 1988). This technique can be used outside the framework of process design but in the presentation which follows in this chapter, we are going to use the concepts and terminology that we have used so far. Specifying the physical means is the last stage of the process design.

METHOD

The physical set-up of the process results from two sets of constraints: the organisational constraints (magnitude, location, people, reporting structure) shown as a vertical axis on Figure 13.1 and the logical model, shown as an horizontal axis on the figure.

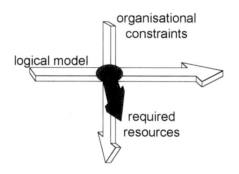

Figure 13.1 Specifying the Physical Resources

Steps

The three steps that we shall follow are:

1) specify the requirements (= the design goals and objectives)

2) search and quantify a sufficient set of options

3) select solutions and plan evolutionary delivery

SPECIFY THE REQUIREMENTS

The most effective way to compile a requirement is through a small series of workshops in which the main stakeholders are represented: the management of the area, the users and the developers or procurers. These workshops should understand the considerations arising from both the logical and organisational ties which are critical for the area under construction or redesign (see Chapters 3 and 4). The facilitator of these workshops should ideally understand well the relevant part of the logical model.

The results should be expressed in business and user terms, not as technical solutions. This document should typically be one to twelve pages long. If more detailed discussions are necessary then they should be relegated to appendices. The direct relationship between purpose and measured attributes should be clear and obvious for a non-technically minded reader. After an initial reaction of disbelief, the participants often find the discipline beneficial, even enjoyable, and acquire an understanding of the vocabulary and concerns of the other stakeholders. This is a by-product of the technique which reinforces good team-working practice.

Capabilities are the Basis of the Requirements

Purpose and goals express the purpose of the organisation as a whole, or of each of its processes, as a capability delivered to its 'customers': for example, 'to support customer engagement' or 'to receive emergency calls'. The goals are sub-clauses of the purpose expressing the refinement of the purpose with respect to relevant considerations (usually the needs of the main stakeholders).

Quantified Capabilities

The objectives are the goals quantified in terms of magnitude and time. They are the capabilities that the organisation need in order to achieve its objectives. (We have consistently used the term *capability* as 'a set of resources in a desirable state', for example: 'available customer engagement facility', or 'a manned emergency desk'.) If too complex, capabilities can be decomposed. For that decomposition, we can use either a concept diagram, as seen in Part III (see Figure 13.2), or a tree decomposition (see Figure 13.3) or simply use a structured list.

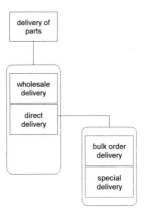

Figure 13.2 Concept Diagram for a Decomposed Capability

The capabilities are 'binary' in nature: they are there or not. For example, 'to record a customer's detail', or 'to manufacture engine parts', or to 'receive emergency calls'. If they are too complex, they can be decomposed: for example, 'to record a customer's detail' can be decomposed into: 'to record a new customer', 'to record on-going transactions with a customer', 'to record the termination of a customer's account'.

On the tree decomposition of Figure 13.3 we see that it is possible to express also the proportion of the various components of a capability.

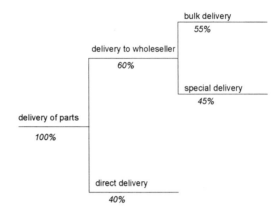

Figure 13.3 Tree Decomposition of a Capability

Capabilities are never developer's options or solutions. 'To have a computer for recording a customer's details' is already expressed as a solution. Capabilities are usually expressed as a verb: 'to ...'. If a solution is a given — 'the operating system will be UNIX' or a policy decision must be followed, e.g. 'the transcription of the original documents will be manual' - then these should be expressed as capabilities in the requirement.

Capabilities are physically made up of activities, people and logistical means. The physical resources include the people and the logistical means necessary for the physical implementation of processes. Their procurement involves the recruitment, training and retraining of the people and the finding, invention or identification of the logistical means — IT systems, communication systems, workflow automation systems — or the traditional logistics i.e. manufacture, transport, storage. The management of the people is preferably undertaken within a competency framework.

Quantified Requirements

The organisation may have already some capabilities and *the object of the procurement task is to bridge the gap between what we have and what we need* (see Figure 13.4); for example, 'to provide a face-to-face customer engagement in all our branches rather than at the main regional offices'. A requirement is not a capability but a *jump in capability*. The difference between capability and requirement may be considered a subtle one but is important to keep in mind.

what we have   what we need

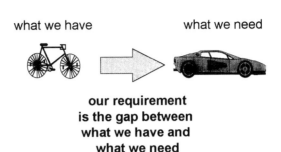

**our requirement
is the gap between
what we have and
what we need**

Figure 13.4 A Requirement is not a Capability

Capability Attributes

The capabilities that we require should be quantified. They are always two conflicting sets of attributes: those that we want to minimise — like cost, time, inconvenience, risk — and those that we want to maximise — like benefits, advantages, ease of use. What we eventually get is always a compromise, the best benefit/cost, or value for money. The rule of the game is to understand the boundaries of the 'compromise field' and to negotiate the best compromise. Because what we get can usually be improved with time and money, we can agree to have something earlier and something better later on. The procurement activity has time as an extra dimension to deal with, in addition to costs and benefits: what, how and when can we have something to start with and what, how and when can we have something better later on. The calendar of delivery is part of the specification.

Figure 13.5 Life Options are Often Compromises Between Good and Evil, Benefits and Costs

Let us clarify and formalise these ideas.

Attribute Levels

The attributes of the capabilities should be measured on a measurable attribute scale. It is always possible to find a scale — a yardstick — to express the intensity or magnitude of these attributes.

What will be of interest to us are four levels on the scale: the current value, the minimum acceptable level, the target value and the best achievable level — the 'blue sky' level — given all favourable conditions, time and money (see Figure 13.6).

We can summarise these concepts on a diagram where the purpose is refined into goals, each goal requires one or several capabilities (see Figure 13.6). Each capability is qualified by its *bonus* and *malus*, or more simply, in *what needs to be maximised* and *what needs to be minimised*.

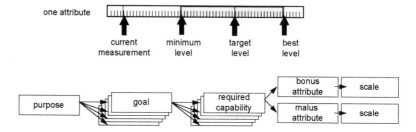

Figure 13.6 Specification Concepts

Compromise Field

A diagram can visualise the field of compromise with the malus (costs) on the horizontal axis and the bonus (performance requiremnts or benefits) on the vertical axis. The values of interest on the bonus scale are: the *minimum acceptable performance*, the level below which the benefit or quality is unacceptable (also called '*maximum acceptable level of pain*') and *the maximum affordable performance*: the level obtained with all the resources available and applying state-of-the-art technology. On the malus scale, the two values of special interest are: the *minimum amount of resources (cost)* to be deployed and the *maximum amount of resources available* (see Figure 13.7).

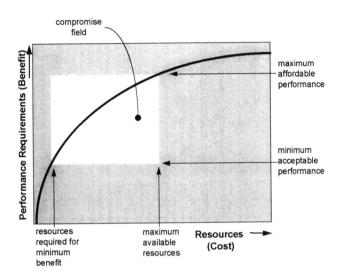

Figure 13.7 The Compromise Field for One Capability

The domain on the diagram bounded by these quantities defines the range of acceptable compromises or the *compromise field*, for short.

In writing specifications, it is unfortunately common practice to provide only one value for each of the target attributes of the required facility: 'the volume of data is 2 GBytes', 'the response of response will be less than 2 seconds'. The provider has only this figure to work from, and the reasoning which has been conducted by the future users before writing down this figure is completely lost. For each improvement, we often find that there is always a range of possibilities and the higher the quality or benefit, the higher the price to pay.

The requirements should be driven by the imperatives from the direction (organisation goals and objectives) and by the outstanding issues (internal and external) as shown on Figure 13.7.

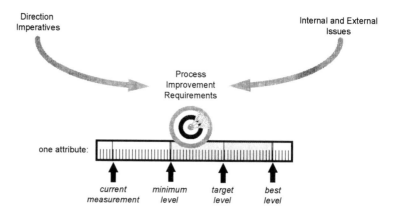

Figure 13.8 Quantification of the Capability Attributes

If we combine the attribute levels of the various capabilities onto one diagram, we obtain a map of the compromises, as on Figure 13.9.

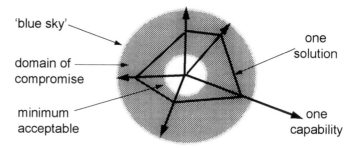

Figure 13.9 The Solutions in the Compromise Field

This map does not have to be actually drawn, but it could become a rule of good practice to do so. This map provides a basis for negotiation between the users (and funders) and the providers, replacing the traditional confrontations between the different parties. Without a visible representation of the compromises, each party might feel that they are always in conflict with the others. The providers also know what is the minimum acceptable, non-negotiable, performance.

This representation of the compromise field — and the reasoning behind it — is also the basis for negotiating an evolutionary delivery. Over time, and with phased funding, the successive improvements on the initial delivery can be plotted, giving the targets for each successive release of the resources.

Attribute Specification

A form can be convenient to capture the table of the critical attributes and their measurements. Figure 13.10 shows a possible layout for such a form (Gilb 1988).

	Attribute	B:Benefit C:Cost	Test	Test Method	Scale/ Unit	Current Value	Min. Value	Target Value	Best Value
1	usability	B	see decompo sition						
2	performance	B	response time	entering one record	seconds	120	30	5	less than 5
3	adaptability	B	time to upgrade	adding a new field	minutes	2 days	60	15	less than 15
4	security	B	access	access control	type of user	none	2 levels	3 levels	3 levels
11	cost	C	cost of developm ent	cost to first user release	$000		30	15	3
12	availability	C	release to users	version 1 release	weeks		6	4	1

Figure 13.10 Attribute Specification Table

Attribute Decomposition

If we have more than ten or twelve critical attributes, it could be better to regroup them into logical chunks. Conversely, we can decompose an attribute which is too difficult to quantify or is too complex. For example, we could decompose *usability* in Figure 13.10 as *speed of learning, speed of making backup of data, speed of recovering from failures*. The quantitative measurements will then be defined only at the decomposed level. There are cases where this is the only practical way of specifying the measurements.

Attribute Decomposition Templates

With time, an organisation will develop its own set of attributes. These sets can be reused as templates for each new problem. Tom Gilb in his publications provides us with some examples of generic templates (Gilb 1988).

For example, the capability attribute 'adaptability' can be decomposed as shown in Figure 13.11.

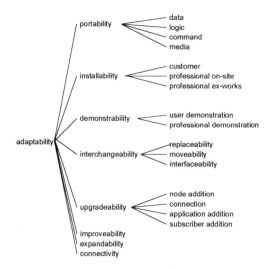

Figure 13.11 Attribute Template for 'Adaptability'

Many terms ending in '... bility' have to be invented in order to capture concepts which are real for describing capabilities but are not always expressed as such.

SEARCH AND QUANTIFY A SUFFICIENT SET OF OPTIONS

Having clarified and documented the requirements, the next step is to find the *solutions*. There is often a whole range of solutions to a particular requirement. This is where the solution providers will be free to explore all the technical alternatives. The attribute specification table is the instrument to be used in order to decide the contribution of each available option. The providers can themselves decide if a particular option is worth presenting to the future users: if the solution does not fall into the compromise field, it is either because it does not meet the minimum level of capability or because it is too expensive (exceeds the maximum allowed resources).

The solutions are any idea, technique, product or measures which affect the attributes. Examples of solutions are: 'every record will receive a unique identifier', 'bonus schemes for employees will be based on team performance', 'all systems will be able to support client-server architecture', 'all legal requirements will be supervised by a central process', 'the transport will be sub-contracted to local firms'.

Solutions are never goals of the users and, as discussed earlier, if they are given they should be specified as capabilities. Solutions are never good or bad in themselves. It is their contribution to the users' objective which should be quantified. They can be traded off with other solutions in order to deliver the total contribution: solution A might potentially deliver only 50% of the requirement but if there is also a solution B which delivers at least the other 50% then A and B will be proposed together. In order to analyse these contributions, it is useful to use a '*solution attribute estimation*' table and an '*impact estimation*' table.

The *solution attribute estimation table* shown in Figure 13.12 shows that the attributes are those selected for the required capabilities (Figure 13.10).

Capability: Recording Customer Details

Solution: System X from ACME Co Ltd

	Attribute	Test	Test Method	Scale/ Unit	Target Level	Esti- mated Level	Uncer- tainty	Reason	Quota of Target Level (%)
1	usability	see decom- position							
2	performanc e	response time	entering one record	seconds	5	10	5	untested solution	50
3	adaptability	time to upgrade	adding a new field	minutes	15	0.5 day	0.5 day	users experien ce	16
4	security	access	access control	type of user	3 levels	3 levels	0		100
1 1	cost	cost of develop ment	cost to first user release	$000	15	12	2	options	80
1 2	availability	release to users	version 1 release	weeks	4	2	0		50

Figure 13.12 Solution Attribute Estimation Table

The same test, test method and scale or units are used. The sixth column shows the target level of performance (the planned value) and the next column shows the estimated degree of uncertainty of that level of performance. This is useful to know because at this stage, the solution might not be completely worked out and we record in the next column the reason for that uncertainty. The next column shows the estimated contribution to the requirement (also a 'guestimate' at this stage).

Such a table will be constructed for each proposed solution. Then a consolidation of the main conclusions — the quota of achievement of the target level — will be undertaken and presented as a summary in the 'combined solution attribute estimation' table. An example is shown on Figure 13.13. The column for 'System X' is transcribed from the solution attribute estimation table for that solution.

Capability: Recording Customer Details							
Solutions:							
	Attribute	System X	Alpha Q	MMM	ABC	CBD	ATMO
1	usability						
2	performance	50	10	100	50	90	83
3	adaptability	16	100	100	90	70	40
4	security	100	100	100	70	100	100
11	cost	125	90	100	150	85	200
12	availability	200	50	70	100	70	100

Figure 13.13 Combined Solution Attribute Estimation Table

Then, from the valid options, the developers would select the optimum solution, or a range of solutions – ideally in co-operation with the users and funders. The next chapter presents an overview of some of the decision analysis techniques which can be used to select between different options.

Having a range of options rather than one single solution is a precondition for discussing an evolutionary delivery. The advantages and principles of such an approach are discussed in the next section.

EVOLUTIONARY PLANNING

Evolutionary planning is a particular type of relationship between suppliers and users who agree to co-operate in the provision of the required capability.

The advantages are early availability of results, better match between the solutions to the needs and, ultimately, savings in terms of money and effort.

This approach is not restricted to the delivery of processes but can be followed in every development project: for example, for a new system, for a new building or for a new training course.

The principles to follow when planning an evolutionary planning are:

1) *small steps of delivery* to users (typically 1 or 2 weeks worth of work, avoiding steps of more than 4 weeks);

2) *something useful* for the user should be delivered by each step — not a mere technical paper, ideally the user should be able to get familiar with it;

3) *limited risk*, the step size should be limited by the degree of risk that we are willing to take;

4) *easy retreat for* each step if it is not successful;

5) *design and build are done in parallel*;

6) *users adjust their perception* of what they actually require - functionality and attributes - as they gain experience and as the environment changes;

7) *developers gain information* about: the real costs, the real meaning of the capabilities, how effective their techniques are.

An example, adapted from a real case, is the planning of software product releases. A development team in discussion with a marketing team created the following list of features for a new release, derived from outstanding enhancements and performance reports:

8) Text browser: single key navigation to next or previous item;

9) Text browser: semantic copy of an entity;

10) Text browser: Windows™ style short cut keys;

11) Graphics editor: semantic copy of an entity;

12) Graphics editor: overview;

13) Graphics editor: full text editing;

14) Graphics editor: single key navigation;

15) Graphics editor: Windows™ style short cut keys;

16) Graphics editor: open by double click;

17) Easier printing function.

The improvements were measured in terms of perceived marketing advantage and cost. The marketing advantage was decided by the marketing team on an arbitrary subjective scale of 0 to 100. The *cost* was the estimated effort in man days for the implementation of each feature. The criteria used to rank the improvements was the ratio of the marketing advantage to the cost. The table on Figure 13.14 shows the result of this analysis in tabular form and Figure 13.15 shows a plot of the cumulative advantage vs. cumulative cost.

No.	Feature	cost	advantage	ratio	cumul. advantage	cumul. cost
1	Text browser: single key navigation to next/previous item	5	30	6	30	5
6	Graphics editor: full text editing	20	90	4.5	120	25
2	Text browser: semantic copy of an entity	30	90	3	210	55
5	Graphics editor: overview	30	80	2.7	290	85
4	Graphics editor: semantic copy of an entity	30	80	2.7	370	115
8	Graphics editor: Windows™ style short cut keys	25	60	2.4	420	140
9	Graphics editor: open by double click	25	70	2.4	490	165
3	Text browser: Windows™ style short cut keys	30	60	2	550	195
7	Graphics editor: single key navigation	90	50	0.6	600	285
10	Easier printing function	70	30	0.4	630	355

Figure 13.14 Table of Incremental Features

The first column is a reference number for the features, the rows are ordered in decreasing order of the ratio advantage over cost (column 5). The cumulative cost shows that the total advantage is 630 (a subjective value) and the cumulative effort is 355 effort-days.

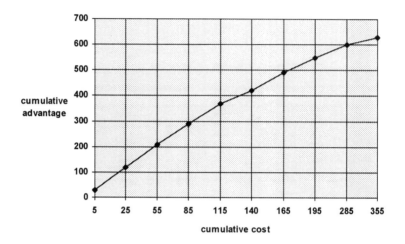

Figure 13.15 Chart of Incremental Features

After examination of the graph, the marketing team decided to have two successive releases of the product by simply dividing the list into two sets of approximately equal costs of 165 and 190 effort-days.

This is a simple application of the evolutionary approach. However, we can be more subtle in deciding the ordering of each successive stage. We could usefully consider the following three criteria:

1) what the *user wants first* — the most useful features (the *'juicy' bits*)

2) what is *easier to do* for earlier results (the *'easy' bits*)

3) what is *logically necessary* to do first (the *'logical' bits*).

The result is a plan of the delivery of the capability over time (see Figure 13.16).

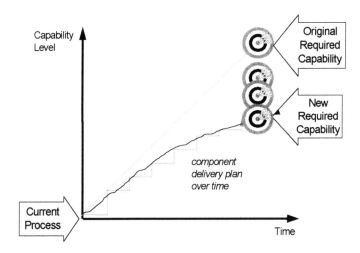

Figure 13.16 Tracking the Requirements

An added benefit of the evolutionary delivery is the ability to revise the original target capability as both users and developers refine their understanding of the requirements. This avoids the common situation where a 'blind' development produces a result that no longer matches the requirements as they stand at the time of the delivery.

SUMMARY

In this chapter we have seen how to specify of the required resources, in the state actually needed to contribute effectively to the business capabilities. Figure 13.17 summarises the method on a diagram.

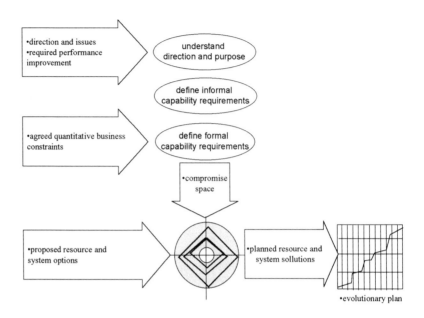

Figure 13.17 The Route Map for the Resource Specification

The starting point is the direction requirements (the tactical plan) and the outstanding issues. From these we define the capability requirements as binary statements ('must be there'). Taking into account the physical parameters of the operation and the wishes of the users - expressed as business constraints - we specify the quantified formal capability requirements. These formal requirements also express the acceptable compromise field into which any solution proposed by the providers should fit. This compromise field also provides the means of planning an evolutionary delivery of the capabilities.

Chapter 14

Influence and Decision Analysis

INTRODUCTION

We make decisions all the time. Although we can handle most of these decisions in our mind without the help of a formal analysis, there are situations where the complexity of the decision domain requires a more systematic approach. This is especially true when we are faced with multiple and conflicting objectives. In these circumstances, an effective solution can be derived from decision analysis, which Larry Philips from the London School of Economics defines as 'an approach and a set of techniques that enable decision makers to examine alternative choices in the face of uncertainty, risk and complexity'.

A good decision is not one which turns out to produce a favourable outcome. Although the research in decision analysis was originally motivated by considering probable future scenarios, we are not interested here in predicting the future. The type of decision analysis that interests us in the context of process design involves considering all the relevant knowledge or opinions in hand at the time of the decision, in order to make choices based on this knowledge and opinions.

In this chapter, we shall consider two types of techniques: *influence analysis* and *decision analysis*.

INFLUENCE ANALYSIS

The cause-effect interdependence between a number of entities is useful to gaining an understanding which:

1) reduces the complexity of a discussion domain, for example in analysing a set of issues or problems, and

2) documents the parameters of a decision problem.

Figure 14.1 shows that entity C depends on entity A and B by drawing an arrow between A and C and between B and C.

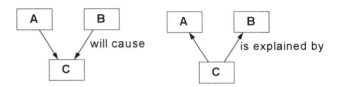

Figure 14.1 Simple Influence Diagrams

The notation can be made more complex to reflect, say, the strength of the influence (Forrester 1975 and Eden and Smihin 1984). The Ithink™ software facility, also called STELLA™, is another example of a derivative notation used for modelling environments such as economic or market domains (Richmond et al 1987). For process design, a simple notation can meet our purpose.

In analysing issues with existing processes, we are often faced with sets of hundreds of issues and we want to find out those issues which are the real causes of the other ones. By constructing the cause-effect network, we can easily identify the *root issues* — those which are not influenced by others, and the *end-effects* — those issues which do not influence others.

The network shown on Figure 14.2 is an example of such an analysis. The root issues are usually very small in number, typically three to twelve. Addressing these root issues will impact all the others. In this hypothetical example, there are only three root issues out of seventeen identified issues. If we address them, we have a good chance to resolve most of the other ones as well. In this hypothetical example, there are only three root issues out of seventeen identified issues. If we address them, we have a good chance to resolve most of the other ones as well.

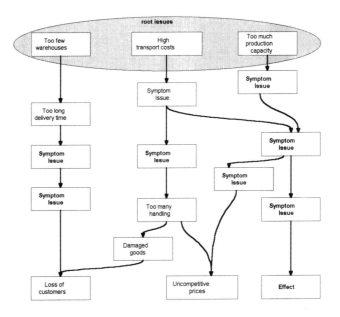

Figure 14.2 Example of an Issue Influence Diagram

Another use for the influence diagram is to analyse the constituent parts of a decision problem and to summarise the analysis in the shape of a decision tree showing the alternative choices leading to alternative paths. For example, Figure 14.3 shows this approach applied to the analysis of a decision involving the options: close a factory in the South; switch transport to rail; or open a distribution centre in the West. In this case, the options which influence the others should be considered first in the decision tree. The resultant influence diagram is shown on the left of Figure 14.3, and the corresponding decision tree on the right.

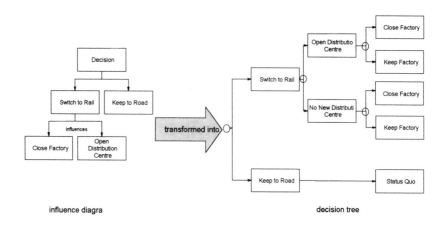

influence diagra   decision tree

Figure 14.3 Influence Diagram and Decision Tree

DECISION ANALYSIS TECHNIQUES

In this section we shall review the relevance of decision analysis, especially *multivariate utility modelling*, to the implementation phase of process design where we have to choose and plan the implementation of the redesigned processes. These solutions require decisions about procedures, people, systems, resource and locations. They must take into account the business priorities and the business constraints such as values, people's attitude and geographical reality.

The rational basis of decision making is now a well-established discipline but is not as widely followed as it should be. Research started in the 1920s but has been confined since the late 1960s to a limited range of applications but is relevant to a wider field (Phillips 1989).

The general process of decision making could follow five broad steps:

1) *structuring*: concerned with the definition of the problem, the identification of the parameters — criteria — of the decision domain (for example, costs and benefits) and the identification of the options (for example, the set of available suppliers);

2) *quantifying*: where we assign values or probabilities to the parameters, in order to express the facts or opinions that we have about each of the options;

3) *evaluating*: where an outcome consistent with the facts and opinions is logically deducted, by hand or with the assistance of a software facility;

4) *deciding*: the best alternative is established, by taking into account the decision maker's attitude to risk — this step is also the opportunity to

review the decision domain and the facts and opinions if the outcome does not 'feel right'; when it would be time to conduct a *sensitivity analysis*;

5) *selling* the proposed decision, this is an optional fifth step — communicating and justifying the outcome to the stakeholders.

The complexity of decision making is caused by the need to cope with both *randomness* and *fuzziness*. Randomness comes from the fact that events, which could effect the outcome of some decisions, may or may not have occurred. Fuzziness is when the factors themselves are unclear, or when the preferences of the decision maker are not totally consistent.

There are well-known statistical techniques for tackling randomness of the components of the decision (Buchanan 1982 and Thomas 1984). In some decision making, the expected outcome could be expressed, for example, as: 'If we follow this plan, we have 45% chance to capture 10% of the market but if we take the other route, we have 25% chance to capture 30% of the market.'

But the difficulty in most management decisions is caused by the fuzziness of the factors and the unclear preferences of the decision maker between different options. The study of fuzziness can be treated scientifically (Zimmerman et al 1984). More simply, management decisions are typically of the form: 'Among the three proposals received for the new system, which supplier is the best, considering cost and long term availability.' The outcome might take a more complicated form: 'The solution is to take component A from supplier X, service B from supplier Y and back-up from supplier Z.'

While data and logical analysis is important for rational decisions, a sound value judgement is necessary to validate the choices. It is then necessary to integrate information analysis and preference analysis in the decision process. The techniques are now well established and can be quite natural and straightforward, although access to the software tools which are also available makes the decision process easier and quicker.

A systematic analysis often reveals hidden interdependence between parameters. If the degree of uncertainty is too high in the eyes of the decision maker, it is possible to reduce the uncertainty about the decision criteria by obtaining additional information, in effect replacing opinions by facts. The profitability of the additional cost — in time or money — in securing a more informed decision must be clarified before spending this additional effort.

Decisions in the management field fall into two distinct classes:

- *single* solution: where there must be only one outcome out of a given set of options;

- a package of solutions - where the outcome is made up of a set of elements which cannot be taken singly.

A single solution problem might be selecting one computer system out of a number of proposed received from different suppliers. A typical example of a package of solutions could be the distribution of a budget between competing projects or departments. In the following sections we shall address these two cases successively.

ANALYSING THE OPTIONS FOR A SINGLE SOLUTION

In this case, we need to select one solution or conclusion out of a fixed set of different options in the face of some degree of uncertainty. The difficulty of doing this is often due to the fact that the decision criteria are often not expressible with the same unit: the criteria could include, for example, Return On Investments (£), market share (%) and future growth (customer satisfaction or number of repeat orders).

The solution is to use the common yardstick of *preference* or, *multi-attribute utility*. A convenient scale should be adopted for a yardstick, usually 0 to 100. The yardstick is applied separately to each of the criteria for each of the options which are considered. If we are consistent in our judgement, then we can take each criterion in turn and assign a value of 0 to the worst option and 100 to the best option, with other options ranked in between usually 0 to 100 (see Figure 14.4).

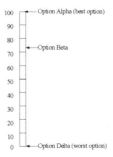

Figure 14.4 Utility Scale for One Criterion

The range of process improvement and re-engineering cases where decision analysis is relevant is wide, covering areas like: looking for the best 'value for money' goods or services, choosing candidates; selecting suppliers, looking for a new site for relocating a business unit; or selecting investment opportunities.

DECISION ANALYSIS STEPS

Step 1. Structuring

The first step is to understand the criteria and the options which will be considered in the decision. The criteria are often broken down into components which are easier to scale. The result is a composition tree of the criteria.

For example, an organisation needs a new computer system and a decision must be made between the offer of different vendors: Delta Plus, Mini data, Regulon and Donovan.

The chosen criteria can be displayed on a decomposition tree as shown on Figure 14.5. The HIVIEW™ software tool was used for creating this decision tree (Krysalis Limited 1994a).

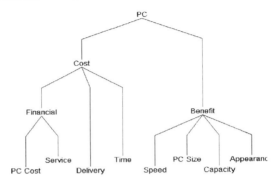

Figure 14.5 Tree of the Decision Criteria

Criteria could fall into two classes:

1) those which must be *minimised*: simply expressed as the 'costs', for example financial (PC cost, delivery cost and service cost) and time (delivery delay);

2) those which must be *maximised*: simply expressed as the 'benefits', for example speed (of processor); PC size (of memory); capacity (of disk); and appearance.

Alternatively, we might want to consider other relevant considerations such as risk. Costs can be money such as capital costs, running costs or recruitment costs but can also be inconvenience, delays, travel time, in fact any attribute that is a necessary constraint. Similarly, benefits can include monetary quantities like Return On Investments or financial saving opportunities but also market share, improved image, comfort, convenience, reliability, growth opportunities. Risk is sometimes considered as a parameter to be minimised although some analysts like to treat it as a third 'dimension' in addition to cost and benefit.

Each criterion is broken down until it can be quantified and is relevant to the decision to be made. For example, reliability can be decomposed into Mean-Time-Between-Failures (MTBF), repair time, minimal loss of data, or any consideration relevant to the situation.

Step 2. Quantifying

The key to a rational decision process is to be able to quantify any criterion which is relevant. Experience shows that there is always a way to measure a criterion. This sometimes requires the application of creative thinking. In the IT field, Tom Gilb has advocated since the 1970s the application of similar rational and creative thinking in specifying systems and his work can be used as a useful source of ideas (Gilb 1988).

If objective values are available, these values can be used and adjusted in order to fit on the 0 to 100 scale — perhaps by using a software package to do the calculation automatically. For example, if the purchase price of computer systems is £1,000 for the cheapest, £3,500 for the most expensive and £1,800 for the third one, then the respective utility values will be 0, 100 and 72. But even without the availability of objective numbers, it is not very difficult to assign numbers on a scale from 0 to 100. With a bit of experience, it is possible to differentiate between options within 3 points on that scale.

The relative importance of the criteria is reflected in a numerical weight which can be assigned to each criterion. Any convenient scale of values can be used. In the example shown on Figure 14.6, four criteria would be assigned the weight 5, 5, 8 and 10. The value 10 is assigned to the criterion with the highest importance ('reliability'); the criteria 'price' and 'running cost' have half that importance (value 5); and 'features' is roughly in between (value 8). Another scale could be more relevant to a different problem, for example 1000, 1000, 1100 and 1250.

For a problem where the criteria and options can be quantified directly, combining the results for all the criteria is a straightforward computation. The score for each option in Figure 14.6, for example (Alpha, Beta, Gamma), is obtained by multiplying each of its utility values by their weight and summing up the results.

	Options	Alpha	Beta	Gamma
Criterion	Weight			
Price	5	0	100	80
Running cost	5	0	100	90
Features	8	100	50	0
Reliability	10	0	100	0
Weighted utility		800	2050	850

Figure 14.6 Decision Matrix

Step 3. Evaluating

Only the leaves of the tree are assigned utility values for each of the options (see Figure 14.7), the best option receiving the value 100, the worst one receiving the value 0. The overall weighted utility for each of the different options is then computed and the results are displayed in various forms for evaluation.

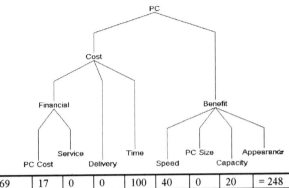

Delta Plus	69	17	0	0	100	40	0	20	= 248
Mini Data	6	0	33	83	0	100	100	60	= 382
Regulon	100	100	100	33	0	60	0	200	= 593
Donovan	0	50	0	100	0	0	99	0	= 249

Figure 14.7 Utility Values for Each Option

If a software facility is used, it will automatically compute the consolidated results for all criteria, taking the weights into account. A tabular presentation shows the result of the analysis and enables to see how the best candidate compares with the other (see Figure 14.8).

Mini-Data vs Delta Plus

○ MDL ORDER   ○ CUMWT   ⊙ DIFF   ○ WTD

Benefit	Capacity	17.4	100	17.39	
Cost	Time	8.3	83	6.94	
Benefit	PC Size	4.3	60	2.61	
Benefit	Appearance	6.5	40	2.61	
Cost	Delivery	4.2	33	1.39	
Financial	Service	6.3	- 17	- 1.04	
Financial	PC Cost	31.3	- 63	- 19.71	
Benefit	Speed	21.7	- 100	- 21.74	
		100.0		- 11.55	

Figure 14.8 Comparison of the Options

A plot of the results according to cost-benefit is a convenient way of analysing the results. The software will produce a cost-benefit map similar to the one shown on Figure 14.9

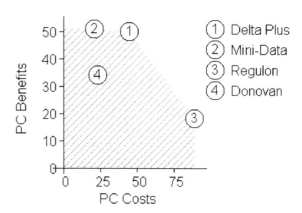

Figure 14.9 Options on the Cost-Benefit Map

Other comparisons can be made in a similar fashion: Costs vs. Risk, or Benefits vs. Risk, for example.

Step 4. Deciding

The software does not make the decision. The results expose the logical consequence of the preferences expressed by the decision makers. At this point, the decision maker can explore the sensitivity of the results to changes that can be made to values and weights and to understand the consequences of the choices. In our example of the choice of a computer system, we may want to see how the outcome is affected if we give the same weights to all the criteria, or if we put more emphasis on the buying cost rather than the long-term costs. Again a software package is a convenient tool to visualise different alternatives.

Decision Analysis Software

In practice, most problems require a larger number of values and tools are more convenient for trying out different sets of values. A software facility can simplify the analysis of complex decisions. This is especially valuable for the facilitation of decision groups where a consensus is required. The analysis of decisions can also be speeded up with tools which offer a fast graphical presentation of the parameters and results, such as HIVIEW. The technique or the software is not a substitute for the decision making proper but they enable the evaluation and justification of the best options.

ANALYSING THE OPTIONS FOR A PACKAGE OF SOLUTIONS

There are many situations where a choice must be made between different packages of solutions rather than between single solutions. It is often difficult to decide between a large number of permutations with no obvious winner. Or there could be conflicts within an organisation which make the decision complex. Another case is when considering an evolutionary implementation of solutions for a business process re-engineering programme. This requires also to consider the value and cost of different packages of solutions. These packages could make up the successive deliveries of the programme. But how do you ensure that the packages with the highest value for money are delivered first?

The need for such packages is common: allocation of a limited R&D budget between several competing projects; deciding on the composition of an investment or marketing portfolio; reorganising sales territories and budgeting with non-financial parameters. The complexity of the decision grows quickly out of control. With four territories, each with four to six options, there are around 500 different permutations. If a couple more areas are added, the number of possibilities to consider can reach 15,000. There is a clear advantage in using a software package to administer this large number of solutions and to examine conveniently the most attractive options.

Package Analysis Software

We can apply the same principles and techniques that we have considered in the previous sections when the outcome was only one choice out of a set of options. However, without the help of a software facility, the complexities of the calculation get quickly out of hand.

Again, a software package also allows the quick exploration of all alternatives and gives an understanding of the sensitivity of the solutions in relation to the preference expressed by the decision makers. For instance, Krysalis Limited's package EQUITY™ for Windows™, supports the approach developed by Larry Phillips in which a group of people who have a solid experience-based understanding of the parameters are brought together in a 'decision conference' (Krysalis Limited 1994b and Phillips 1984). These are used to create and agree the model on which to base the selection of optimum solutions or packages of solutions. In such a situation, the software must not get in the way of the interactions in the group. The next section shows a short extract of a hypothetical, but typical, case study.

EXAMPLE OF PACKAGE ANALYSIS: ALLOCATION OF MARKETING RESOURCES

The problem posed to the decision makers in this example is to consider different ways of increasing sales by changing the allocation of resources in the customer engagement process. The business is a company supplying telecommunications services, which involves managing a number of business accounts.

A range of possibilities — including reducing the budget in a particular activity — can be considered. In most decision making situations, keeping the 'status quo', in this case keeping the budget allocations as they are, is always one of the options.

It was decided to break up the customer engagement process into the four activities in the life-cycle of a customer account:

1) *MARCOM (Marketing and Communication)*: raising awareness through marketing campaign;

2) *Sales:* transforming enquiries into accounts;

3) *Account Management*: ensuring that subscribers are taking full advantage of the offered services;

4) *Post Mortem*: understanding the reason for termination of accounts and possibly recovering custom.

For each activity, a varying number of options are considered, as discussed in the following subsections:

Activity: MARCOM

- Reduced level: cut campaign budget

- Focused level: direct campaigns at priority user groups

- National level: use national undifferentiated campaigns only

- National and focused level: direct national and focused campaigns at specific user groups

Activity: Sales (Response process for campaigns)

- Mail level: mail only

- Telephone level: telephone sales desk

- All level: all means of receiving orders

Activity: Account Management (Management of the signed up subscribers)

- None level: no specific monitoring of account activities

- Circular level: regular promotion using circulars

- Monitor level: automatic monitoring of account activities

- Focused level: focused promotions to selected accounts

Activity: Post Mortem

- None level: no post mortem

- Mail level: mail follow-up

- Phone level: individual inquiries by phone

This decision model can be displayed on a diagram as on the screen dump in Figure 14.10. The activity 'Sales' is highlighted on that particular screen.

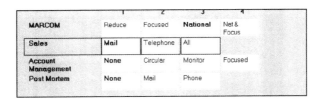

	1	2	3	4
MARCOM	Reduce	Focused	**National**	Net & Focus
Sales	**Mail**	Telephone	All	
Account Management	None	Circular	Monitor	Focused
Post Mortem	None	Mail	Phone	

Figure 14.10 The Decision Model

For each option, the decision group or the individual decision maker would determine an approximate level of cost and benefit, refined as required into more detailed measurements. Cost could, for example, be expressed as set-up cost and running cost. Other examples could include:

- next-year operating costs;

- following year operating costs;

- capital expenditure;

- research personnel required.

Benefits could be increased business, reduced attrition level and increased number of subscribers. But benefits could also be expressed as for example:

- revenue over next three years;

- expected market share in two years;

- estimated profit in three years;

- fit with the organisation mission;

- growth potential.

It is also possible to attach weights to the criteria in order to reflect the relative importance given to the different criteria.

There is a natural tendency to be too detailed. The best approach is to select enough attributes to represent the concerns of the decision makers but no more. Two to five attributes should be sufficient.

The software can display the various solutions as packages of options (one for each area) as shown on Figure 14.11.

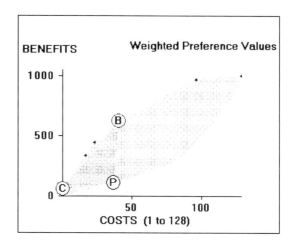

Figure 14.11 The Computed Options on a Benefits/Costs Diagram

The currently proposed solution (often the 'status quo') is indicated with the symbol 'P'. There are almost always two better solutions: a cheaper one with similar or higher benefits indicated with the symbol 'C' and a better one which with a minimum increase in cost would deliver a much higher benefit, indicated on the diagram by the symbol 'B'.

Sensitivity analysis is performed by refining the estimates of cost and benefits and by considering alternative options in the order of increased benefit/cost ratio. A list of 'buy' or 'sell' is used for that purpose as shown in the 'buy' list in Figure 14.12.

	AREA	LEVEL	COSTS	Cumulative COSTS	BENEFITS	Cumulative BENEFITS
0	1 MARCOM	1 Reduce	1	1	0	0
0	2 Sales	1 Mail	0	1	0	0
0	3 Account Mgt	1 None	0	1	0	0
0	4 Post Mortem	1 None	0	1	0	0
1	4 Post Mortem	2 Mail	1	2	56	56
2	2 Sales	3 All	16	18	282	338
3	4 Post Mortem	3 Phone	7	4	103	441
4	1 MARCOM	2 Focused	7	41	177	618
5	3 Account Mgt	4 Focused	55	96	352	971
6	1 MARCOM	4 Nat & Focus	3	128	29	1000

Figure 14.12 Allocation of Marketing Resources in Order of 'Best Buy'

This type of analysis is not a substitute for the discretion of the decision makers. With the results of the analysis in hand, the decision makers can test their 'gut' feeling and change the criteria, values and weights and see immediately the consequences of these changes. Experience shows that the software analysis provides invaluable insight into the decision model and reveals opportunities which were not obvious at the onset.

EVOLUTIONARY DELIVERY

The 'best buy' order can also be used to determine further improvements to the process. The first cut of the additional projects in the evolution can be derived from a list produced by analysing the increasing benefits and costs created by including further options. Planning the actual project requires the consideration of other constraints, such as operational inconvenience, resource availability, marketing programmes and budgets.

In the example in Figure 14.12, the initial best package consists of:

- reducing the budget in MARCOM;
- keeping a mail-only sales support;
- having no account management;
- having no post-mortem.

The next best improvements, in order of diminishing returns are:

1) sending a letter to terminating accounts (mail post-mortem);
2) supporting all types of sale support (mail, telephone, fax, email);
3) calling up terminating accounts (phone post-mortem);
4) performing focused MARCOM campaigns;
5) focusing promotions for managed accounts;
6) performing focused as well as national MARCOM campaigns.

CONCLUSIONS

The use of these decision techniques can speed up considerably the planning of improvements and re-engineering.

The decision analysis techniques that we have reviewed are especially relevant during two of the four generic phases of process redesign:

1) WHAT: Focus for redesign,
2) HOW: Searching for solutions and evolutionary implementation planning.

They should facilitate the work of a design team and shift the discussion from subjective and emotive arguments to documented and objective reasons. Hidden opportunities can also be uncovered and can be readily explored, such as packages of solutions which were not obviously apparent.

———————————————— Part V

References

Chapter 15

Summary of the *a*BC*d* Techniques

OVERVIEW OF THE TECHNIQUES

Most of the techniques used in this book are integrated into the '*applied Business Concepts design*' (*a*BC*d*™) method, an approach developed for undertaking business improvement projects by Business Concepts *international* Limited. In practice, it is more efficient to use a computer-based package to record the models and to produce the diagrams. Developers are encouraged to create software tools to support *a*BC*d*, especially integrated suites. There is no royalties expected but this book should be mentioned as the reference for the method. This chapter summarises the notation used in for the diverse techniques in *a*BC*d*. Figure 15.1 shows the relationship between the techniques and the diagrams.

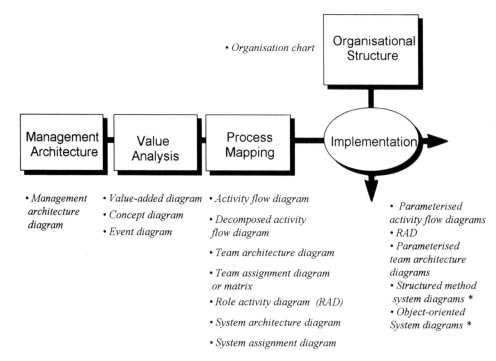

Figure 15.1 Techniques and Diagrams for Process Design and Improvement

ORGANISATIONAL STRUCTURE

The organisational structure is the 'vertical dimension'. It documents the visible organisation at a given time. This structure tends to change very quickly (sometimes every week).

The Organisation Chart

The organisation chart is designed to show reporting structure (the people) and the geographical reporting structure. The organisation chart does not explain how the organisation works. There are many conventions used for this type of chart. The following is one example.

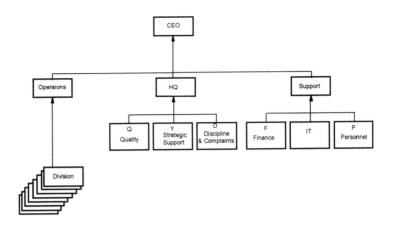

Figure 15.2 Example of Organisation Diagram

MANAGEMENT ARCHITECTURE

The 'horizontal' logical dimension is concerned with the abstract, reusable templates for management and operational processes. The management architecture is one of three aspects of logical dimension, the value analysis is the second one, concerned with the logical processes and the last one, process mapping, is used to model the generic implementable processes.

The generic management architecture describes how an organisation defines its mission, goals, objectives and required capabilities and how it procures and manages its capabilities.

The Management Architecture Diagram

The *management architecture diagram* shows the relationship between the three levels of Management Processes (see Figure 15.3):

1) Direction management process or DMP (Strategy);

2) Capability management process or CMP (Tactics and management of the means);

3) Operation management process or OMP (Implementation or operation).

The management architecture diagram does not show the organisation as depicted on a typical organisation chart but rather a generic management structure.

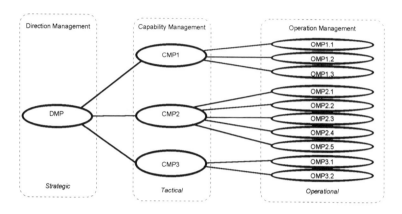

Figure 15.3 Management Architecture Diagram

The lines between the management processes indicates a common set of considerations which are best implemented by sharing some roles which are specially responsible for these considerations. Some prefer to show this relationship by overlapping the processes as on Figure 15.4. In practice, with many overlaps, the diagram can become difficult to read.

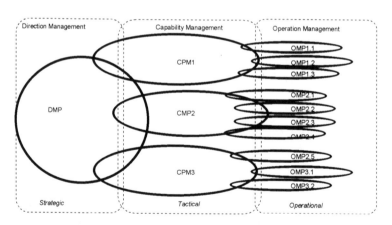

Figure 15.4 Management Architecture Diagram (Overlapping Processes)

VALUE ANALYSIS

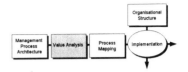

The value analysis defines the components of the capabilities, the relevant concepts, the sub-types of these concepts and their states.

Value-Added Diagram

The *value-added diagram* shows the decomposition of a concept into its constituents (see Figure 15.5). This decomposition is used to understand the make-up of the end-product or end-service of an organisation, a function or a system in terms of other products or services.

On the diagram, the systems or processes delivering the products are also shown. As a rule, a process only delivers one end-product.

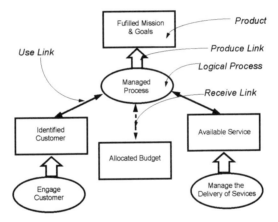

Figure 15.5 Simple Example of a Value-Added Diagram

The product of one process is also a 'resource' for another, so we can also consider a product as a 'capability' for the receiving process. As we have defined elsewhere a capability to be a set of resources in a particular state, it is more convenient and more consistent to express the products on the value-added diagram as products in a given desirable state: 'available service' and not just 'service'.

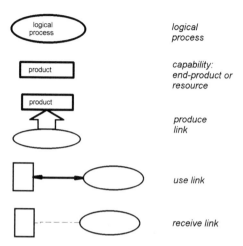

Figure 15.6 Nodes and Links on a Value-Added Diagram

The nodes on the value-added diagram are as follows (see Figure 15.6):

- *process* (logical process);
- *capability* (can be a product or a resource).

The relationships are (see Figure 15.6):

- *produce* (a process produces a product or several by-products);
- *use* (a process uses one or several resources, or none at all);
- *receive* (a process is given a capability that it does not specify).

These relationships are like highways: they support communication and movement of resources in both directions.

Concept Diagram

The *concept diagram* (see Figure 15.7) is a kind of 'semantic net' or 'concept map' which shows the concepts of interest in the domain of discourse under study.

A good concept diagram is simple and even elegant, reflecting the clarity of the concepts. The designer always looks for reductions, simplifications and abstractions in order to achieve the highest possible degree of resilience to changes and new cases. The richness of the diagram comes from its ability to cope with new cases and its support in inducing new relationships through generalisation.

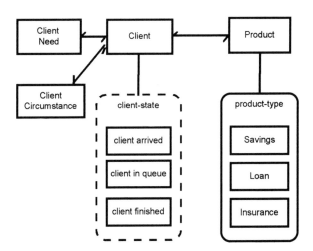

Figure 15.7 Example of a Concept Diagram

The components of the concept diagram are (see Figure 15.8):

- *concept type* or simply *concept*;

- *concept sub-type partition or simply concept partition*, itself containing more concepts which are all *sub-types* of the partitioned concept (a mutually exclusive set);

- *state partition* containing possible states of the super-type (also a mutually exclusive set).

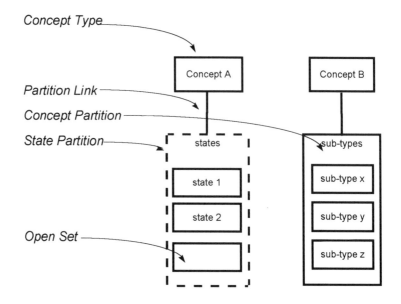

Figure 15.8 Concept Diagram and Components

The possible relationships between concepts are shown in (Figure 15.9).

- *partition link* between a super-concept and one or several partitions (see Figure 15.8);

- *property link* between two concepts, which can have a separate existence, they do not rely on each other for existence (see Figure 15.9).

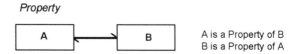

Figure 15.9 Property on an Concept Diagram

- *composition* or '*part-of*' relationship between a composed concept and its components (see Figure 15.10);

- *implication* between only two concepts — the simplest case of a composition (see Figure 15.10).

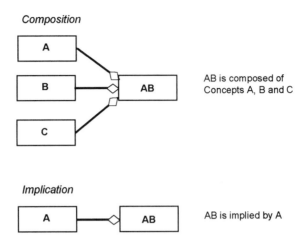

Figure 15.10 Compositions on an Concept Diagram

Event Diagram

The *event diagram* shows the dynamic dependence between *event types* or simply *events* (as shown in Figure 15.11).

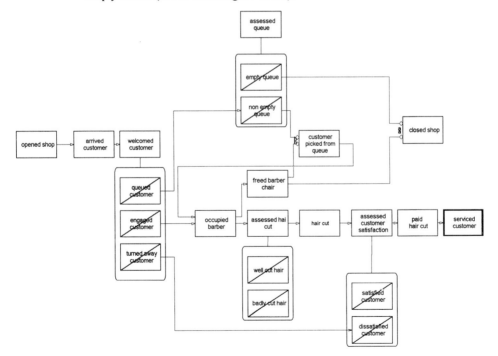

Figure 15.11 Example of an Event Diagram

The nodes on the event diagram (see Figure 15.12) are *events*. They are the *states* of the concepts.

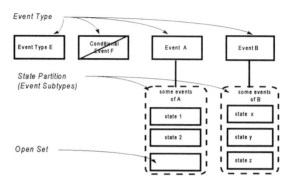

Figure 15.12 Nodes on an Event Diagram

- *State partition*: sub-type of an event, where the occurrence of any of the sub-types implies the occurrence of the super-type. All the states of a concept are not always shown — only those of interest in the context under study.

- *Conditional event*: if the occurrence of the event is conditional, this is shown as a diagonal line across the event.

The relationships on the event diagram are:

- *State partition link* (see Figure 15.12) between an event and each of its partitions;

- *Trigger*: the occurrence of an instance of one event triggers a process which, after a while, results into the occurrence of a new event (see Figure 15.13).

 trigger link

Figure 15.13 Links on an Event Diagram

It is also possible to express batches of triggers (see Figure 15.14).

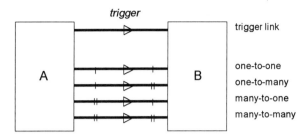

Figure 15.14 Batches on a Event Diagram

The meaning of the batches is a follows:

- *One-to-one*: each occurrence of event A triggers B;

- *Many-to-one*: a predetermined number of events A must occur in order to trigger event B;

- *One-to-many*: a batch of events A are expected to occur, where each one will trigger B as they occur;

- *Many-to-many*: a series of batches of event A are expected to trigger B, could occur in practice but is rather complex.

Several triggers can end up on one event: this is an *OR combination of triggers* (see Figure 15.15).

This modelling technique - composition of events - is useful to express the synchronisation of several event streams on one event. The model does not support the timing of the events, only that several events have to occur in order to achieve synchronisation.

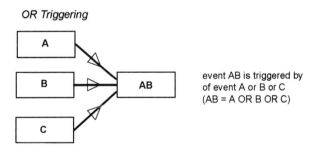

Figure 15.15 Logical OR Triggering of Events

Several triggers can be combined in configuration similar to a composition on the event: this is an *AND combination of triggers* (see Figure 15.16) which is used to synchronise several event streams.

Synchronisation Triggering

A

B —————◇— AB

C

event AB is triggered when
events A and B and C
have occured
(AB = A AND B AND C)

Figure 15.16 Logical AND Triggering of Events

PROCESS MAPPING

Process mapping is concerned with the description of the generic, implementable processes which 'package' the capabilities and concepts into reusable and combinable business components.

Activity Flow Diagram

The *process mapping* and *modelling* of actual or possible implementations are documented with *activity flow diagrams*. Figure 15.17 shows the main activities considered for an implementable solution. In this mapping, there is no distinction between '*activity*' and '*process*'. For convenience, we shall use the term 'activity' for the nodes.

Each activity can be decomposed to a higher level of detail with *decomposed activity flow diagrams*, if this is required for the clarity of the documentation or the design. The details of an activity are shown as a diagram containing its sub-activities. This decomposition can be repeated down to the required level of detail.

The nodes and links on the Activity Diagrams are shown on Figure 15.17.

The nodes are (see Figure 15.18):

- *activity also known as a business process* to distinguish it from a logical process in Value Analysis;

- *external agent or process*: an agent, process or activity outside the scope of the current diagram which initiate or receive information or material;

- *action*: a specific activity;

- *decision*: if there are alternative paths following this activity;

- *input/output*: data, documents, products, material produced or needed by the activities;

- *external activity or external process*: exists outside the scope of the current diagram.

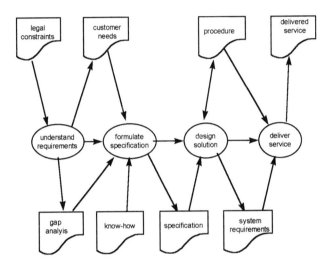

Figure 15.17 Activity Flow Diagram

The links on the Activity Flow Diagram are:

- *input/output (I/O) flow*: between an activity and an I/O in one direction only, the activity either uses or produces the I/O;

- *recursive I/O* flow when the I/O is updated by an activity;

- *dependency/sequencing*: between activities or decisions, indicates that an activity (or decision) can only start after another one has started, no constraint is put on the need to terminate the first activity before starting the second one.

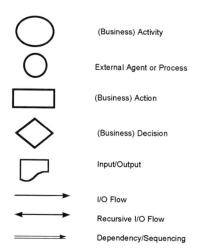

Figure 15.18 Nodes and Links on an Activity Flow Diagram

Decision Modelling

Decisions are usually considered at the most detailed level of documentation of process mapping. By convention, decisions are represented by a diamond-shaped node on the activity flow diagram (see Figure 15.19).

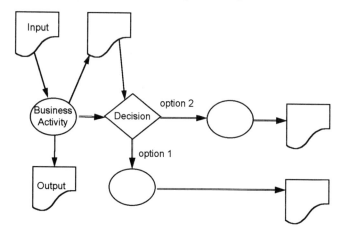

Figure 15.19 Decision on an Activity Flow Diagram

The symbols are the same as in the activity flow diagrams described in the previous section.

Team Architecture Diagram

The composition of the generic teams, in terms of roles, is shown on a *team architecture diagram* (see Figure 15.20).

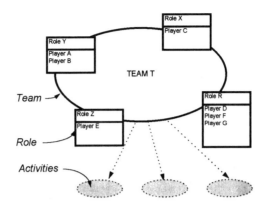

Figure 15.20 Team Architecture Diagram

The same diagram can be used in the implementation phase, when actual names or ranks can be indicated.

Showing the activities on the same diagram is optional. Figure 15.21 shows the nodes which appear on the team architecture diagrams, in two flavours: with and without the indication of the competencies (capability in process parlance) required from the team.

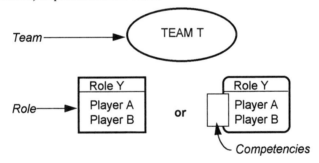

Figure 15.21 Notation on Team Architecture Diagrams

Team Assignment

The assignment of teams to activities is shown as an *assignment diagram* and a *matrix* (see Figure 15.22 and 15.23). The diagram can also show at the same time the required capabilities to meet the objectives. The capabilities are defined by the tactical plan.

The teams 'inherit' the objectives and quality measurements from the activities for which they are responsible.

Team Assignment

The assignment of teams to activities is shown as an *assignment diagram* and a *matrix* (see Figure 15.22 and

Capabilities	Act. 1	Act. 2	Act. 3	Act. 4	Act. 5	Act. 6
objective A			X		X	
objective B		X				
objective C				X		
objective D	X					X
objective E		X				X

Teams	Act. 1	Act. 2	Act. 3	Act. 4	Act. 5	Act. 6
team A	X		X			
team B		X				
team C				X		
team D					X	X

Figure 15.23). The diagram can also show at the same time the required capabilities to meet the objectives. The capabilities are defined by the tactical plan.

The teams 'inherit' the objectives and quality measurements from the activities for which they are responsible.

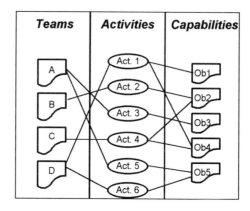

Figure 15.22 Team Assignment Diagram

If a matrix representation is preferred, the diagram must be split into two matrices: *a team assignment matrix* and an *activity measurement matrix* (see Figure 15.23). The matrix is not as graphically appealing as the diagram but it can show the contribution of each activity to the capability objectives. We note that a team may be responsible for several activities but an activity should be assigned to only one team.

Capabilities	← Activities →					
	Act. 1	Act. 2	Act. 3	Act. 4	Act. 5	Act. 6
objective A			X		X	
objective B		X				
objective C				X		
objective D	X					X
objective E		X				X

Teams	← Activities →					
	Act. 1	Act. 2	Act. 3	Act. 4	Act. 5	Act. 6
team A	X		X			
team B		X				
team C				X		
team D					X	X

Figure 15.23 Activity Measurement and Team Assignment Matrices

Role Activity Diagram

The modelling of the detailed interaction between roles can be advantageously documented with the help of *role activity diagrams* or RADs. The example on Figure 15.24 shows an example of RAD.

The assignment of activities to the physical business units can be documented in the implementation phase with RAD.

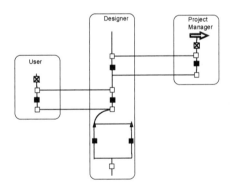

Figure 15.24 Example of Role Activity Diagram (RAD)
(reproduced with the kind permission of Praxis plc, from Ould 1995)

Figure 15.25 shows the notation on RAD diagrams is as follows (Ould 1995). The main nodes are

- *role*;
- *activity*;
- *state description*;
- *start of a role*;
- *external event*.

The main links are:

- *interaction* between roles;
- *concurrent paths* between roles;
- *conditional paths*.

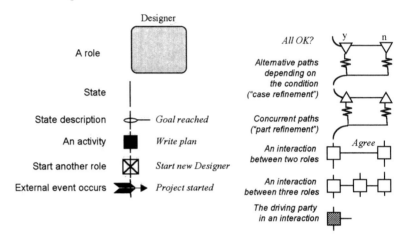

Figure 15.25 RAD notation
(reproduced with the kind permission of Praxis plc)

The RAD notation is specially suitable for the detailed design of procedures and automated processes (workflow automation).

System Architecture Diagram

The supporting systems can be shown on a *system architecture diagram* (see Figure 15.26).

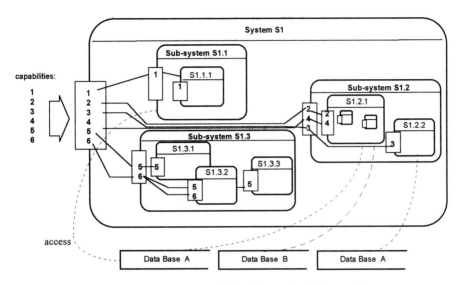

Figure 15.26 System Architecture Diagram

The symbols on the *system architecture diagram* are as follow. The nodes are:

- *system* or *sub-system*: use the same symbols to show a nested architecture, which includes the name of the system or sub-system, with the provided capabilities represented in a box on the side of the symbol and any nested sub-systems;

- accessed *databases* or other external resources.

The links are:

- *capability* links;

- *access* links to databases (information flows) or external resources (information or material).

System Assignment

The assignment of systems to activities is shown as a *system assignment diagram* and/or *a matrix* (see Figure 15.27 and Figure 15.28). The diagram can also show at the same time the required capabilities to meet the objectives (or quality measurements). The capabilities are defined by the tactical plan.

The systems 'inherit' the objectives and measurements from the activities that they support.

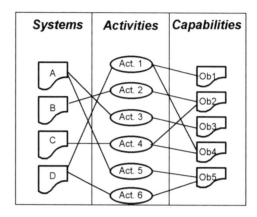

Figure 15.27 System Assignment Diagram

If a matrix representation is preferred, the diagram must be split into two matrices: *a system assignment matrix* and an *activity measurement matrix* also mentioned when discussing team assignments (see Figure 15.28). The matrix can show an estimate of the contribution of each activity to the objectives. We note that a system may be supporting several activities and an activity can use several systems.

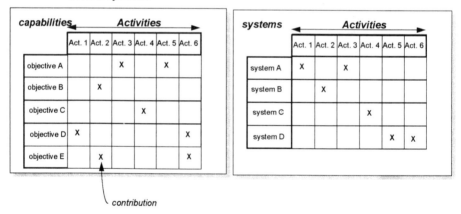

contribution

Figure 15.28 Activity Measurement and System Assignment Matrices

These diagrams can be used as part of the specification of the physical systems. The developers or procurers of these systems will then use specialised techniques and notations for the actual procurement of these resources.

IMPLEMENTATION

In the third dimension, the implementation, the generic implementable processes documented in the process mapping are physically created where they are needed and in as many instances as required by the organisation structure. For example, there can be many hundreds of implementations of the generic process 'open an account', each being constrained by the local business and operational conditions

Each specialist implementation team will use the techniques and notations which are most appropriate for the tasks. However, in order to ensure a rigorous continuity between the process mapping and the implementation, the process mapping diagrams should be used as specification documents for the implementation projects. It is possible to complement these diagrams with the data derived from the organisational structure (the business and operational constraints). Some examples are shown in the following sections.

Parameterised Activity Flow Diagrams for Implementation

It is possible to show the numerical attribute of each process and activity on the activity flow diagrams, although there is a risk of overloading the diagram. The attributes can also be presented in separate tables. For the implementation project, attributes such as authorities, quantity and cost of each resource, set-up time and unit duration time could be considered.

Role Activity Diagrams

RADs can be used as design documents for automating the workflows.

Parameterised Team Architecture Diagram

The generic diagrams can be completed with the name of actual players or ranks.

Systems Diagrams

Each implementation team will use the specialised notation most adapted to their way of working. In the case of bought-in systems, the generic architecture diagrams will be part of the tendering documents. For OO developments, the Value Analysis provides the data from which candidate business objects which will be constructed.

Chapter 16

Glossary

The following are definitions of important words used in process design. Some are commonly used words used every day, but with a slightly different or less precise meaning. The terms are listed in alphabetical order.

abstraction

To ignore most details in a reasoning in order to capture the essence of the subject — achieved by observing or imagining many instances of the same thing and by ignoring distinguishing details.

> *Examples: 'person' as an abstraction used by a personnel department for 'employee', 'supervisor' and 'secretary', or a 'service population' for a hospital as an abstraction of 'registered patients', 'injured travellers', 'to-be born babies' or 'deceased persons'.*

action

The component of a process always resulting in the same result, as opposed to a *decision* which may not always produce the same result.

activity

A particular implementation of a process; what an organisation or a system performs to meet its purpose.

> *Examples: managing in-patients at a hospital; seat reservations for British Airways; sales ledgers for AT & T; training for a police force.*

'Activity' can also be used to designate tasks which are the element of a *process*. A process has a well-defined outcome (delivering a capability) whereas activities may only be described by the *actions* or *decisions* which are undertaken.

bonus

> Something that we want to maximise, expressed as benefits or performance requirements.

business design project

> See *project*.

business improvement project

> See *project*.

business plan

> The integrated plan for the organisation which shows how the *goals* will be achieved.

business process

> A collection of activities identified by a common business purpose which could be implemented across several *business units*. A business unit usually takes part in several business processes.
>
> > *Examples: order processing, procurement, burglary investigation, risk management.*
>
> A business process is a particular implementation of a set of logical processes, characterised by a number of physical and business constraints. Also called *physical process*.

business process design

> The design of the organisation which determines the way it will deliver products and services to customers. The elements of the design are expressed as *mission, process architecture, capabilities, implemented activities, roles* and *logistical means* and the means of measuring the *contribution*.

business process re-engineering

> BPR is an improvement philosophy. It aims to achieve step improvements in performance by redesigning the processes through which an organisation operates, maximising their value-added contents and minimising everything else. This approach can be applied at an individual level or to the whole organisation (Peppard and Rowland 1995).

business unit

> A collection of activities identified by a common functional and a common organisational (location or reporting) relationship. A business unit can be sub-divided into smaller business units. The names given to business units vary

from one organisation to another: Division, Branch, Business Area, Geographical Area, Function, Logical Functional Unit (LFU).

For example: a clinic, a hospital, the purchase department, the research department, the database management system, the Northern area.

capability

A set of resources in a particular desirable state which is required to achieve the objectives of the organisation, or delivered to a customer, another process or another organisation. The requirement for the capability of an organisation is derived from its chosen tactics (the 'WITH' of the organisation). See also *value*.

Capability Management Process

The process responsible for creating one of the core processes identified by the *Direction Management Process*, and for managing its contribution to the *objectives*.

change program

See *continuous improvement* and *strategy*.

class

An instance of an *object type*.

competency

Capability of an individual or a team in the form of personal knowledge, skills, experience and behaviour relevant to the fulfilment of a role in a process.

concept

An instance of a *concept type*.

concept type

A *entity type* used in the description of a process.

continuous improvement

The approach used to monitor the quantitative and qualitative performances of the organisation; to identify the required improvements; and to implement a *change programme*. Such improvements are best implemented as a series of managed steps, the magnitude of which depends on the needs and the dynamism of the organisation.

core capabilities

> The *capabilities* that the organisation needs to achieve its *objectives*.

core processes

> The processes which deliver the *core capabilities* needed by the organisation.

critical success factor (CSF)

> See *key performance indicator*.

customer requirement

> What customers need, now and in the future, the match between customers' requirements and the ability of the organisation to deliver is the prime component of the tactical management of *capabilities*.

customer satisfaction

> The extent to which customers are satisfied with the existing relationship with the organisation can be measured in an ascending scale such as:
>
> 1) satisfied with the existing relationship;
>
> 2) will be fulfilled by other requirements from the organisation;
>
> 3) will recommend others to fulfil their requirements from the organisation.

decision

> The element of a process resulting in none or one of several possible outputs.

delivery

> The means by which either products or services are provided to customers.

direction

> The considerations which are described by the organisation *mission, goals* and *strategy*. The prime responsibility for the direction of the organisation lies with the team in the *Direction Management Process*.

Direction Management Process

> The process responsible for managing the outcome of the organisation, formulating its overall mission, goals and objectives. The DMP identifies the core processes and monitors their performance.

entity

> An instance of an entity type — of particular interest are entities such as: *concept, realm, object, object type, relation, action, decision, event, event type, trigger, production rule.*

entity type

> An abstract notion which describes a set of similar concepts or percepts (existing or imaginary entities of the perceived world).

ethical rule

> A *procedure* which applies to all situations, 'a simple rule for making decisions in complex situations' (Beckett 1995). See *ethics.*

event type

> The creation of an instance of a entity type — in practice, it is usual to use the same identifier for the two notions of event type and *entity type* because there are two ways of expressing the same thing from a static or a dynamic point of view.

> > *For example: the entity type 'invoice' may have a sub-type 'raised invoice', which, in generic terms, results from the process type 'raise invoice'. When the raising of a particular invoice (i.e. the creation of an instance of the type 'raised invoice') occurs, we say that we see the instance of the general event type 'invoice raised'.*

goal

> An aspect of the mission with respect to a particular consideration, including the needs of stakeholders such as customers, employees, shareholders — as well as others like suppliers and the wider community. A goal is not an objective, neither quantified nor timed.

guideline

> A non-prescriptive *procedure.*

impact monitoring

> The factual analysis and measurement in both qualitative and quantitative terms of the impact on the organisation of:

> 1) external events and constraints;

> 2) actual organisation activities;

> 3) aggregate customer behaviour in relation to the delivered products or services.

implementable process

A process described as a generic and reusable organisational component by: a set of logical processes; the *capabilities* provided to other processes; its own capabilities; a team description; and *quality* measurements. This defines all the resources required to implement the process: procedures, roles, the supporting systems, and the performance measurements.

Examples: application processing, order satisfaction, policing a neighbourhood district.

improvement programme

An integrated set of improvement *projects* which relates to the organisation *mission* and *strategy* to achieve the *goals* over a given period of time.

individual contribution

The result of the activity of an individual towards the *objectives* of the organisation, usually as part of a team, by the provision of a set of *competencies*.

instance

A member of a set.

key performance indicator (KPI)

An instrument for measuring and for monitoring the achievements towards the organisation *objectives*, see also *critical success factor*.

logical process

A process described from an abstract point of view by a well-defined domain which defines completely its view of the outside world — its relationships with other logical processes. Within the domain, the process is completely defined by a set of *entity types, concept types, event types* and their relationships. The logical process is usually justified by an end-*event* which can give its name to the process.

Examples: validated application, satisfied customer, controlled threat.

logistical means

The resources used by people to enact a process: including tools, plants, IT systems, communication systems, manufacturing, warehousing and transport facilities.

malus

Something that we want to minimise, for example costs or times.

management process

The way the organisation is managed which, like any other processes, is implemented through activities — but also includes a number of formal communications (meetings) which are concerned with defining, managing, evaluating and improving the business processes.

market development

The development of products and services in line with *customer requirements* achieved through understanding existing and anticipating future customer requirements in order to identify and select market segments — and then to select those products and services which best meet the customer requirements and develop the brand in accordance with the *mission*.

market segment

A set of *customer requirements* which share common attributes.

meta model

A formal generic expression of the *concepts* and the relationships between the concepts, which is relevant to a defined domain of discourse, encompassing all the necessary concepts used to describe the domain.

mission

The expression of the *raison d'être* of the organisation and of the type of products or services delivered to customers. This is usually captured in a public mission statement. The mission is managed by the Direction Management Process.

object

An instance of object type.

object type

An abstraction which corresponds to physical or non-physical *entities*. Physical objects could include 'car', 'telephone', 'people' and 'invoice'; typical examples of non-physical objects that exist in a computer memory are 'number', 'data' and 'money'.

In this book, the more general notion of *entity type* rather than object type is used in discussions. See also *concept* and *class*.

objective

What the organisation needs to do by a given time in order to meet and sustain its *mission* — in the form of an expression of a *goal* or part of a goal, qualified by a level of service and a time scale for its achievement, perhaps including a series of timed achievements. Organisation's objectives are sometimes described as qualitative or quantitative, but as they should always be measurable, the distinction between quantitative and qualitative is not sustainable in practice.

Operation Management Process

The process responsible for using and managing the *capabilities* (the resources) made available by a *Capability Management Process* in order to contribute to the organisation *objectives*.

physical process

A process of a given organisation, implemented in a particular location by a specific team of assigned individuals.

Examples: the application department at head office of ABC company; the order department of XYZ department store; the police squad in NYZ district.

policy

A type of *goal*, expressed as a stance, a viewpoint or a position, contributing to the *direction* of the organisation, applying the *values* of the organisation to a particular consideration or issue.

procedure

A set of rules to apply in particular situations:

* if the procedure is prescriptive ('should'), it is a *production rule*;

* if the procedure is non-prescriptive ('could' rather than 'should'), the procedure becomes a *guideline*;

* if the rules apply to all situations, there are *ethical rules*.

process

A set of purposeful activities, performed by agents, supported by *logistical means*.

Examples: order satisfaction, product development, training course development.

process contribution

The result of the enactment of a process towards the *objectives* of the organisation through the provision of a process *capability*.

processor

> The set of *production rules* which define a process. Once triggered, a processor is expected to complete in a relatively short time period, and terminate in just one (or no) event except in the case of failure or exception.
>
> *Examples: record a patient, discharge patient, check availability of operating room, start engine, stop engine.*

product

> The set of deliverables which are necessary to meet the requirements of customers. In process design, it is also synonymous with capability delivered or required.

production rule

> The description of how and with what an *action* or a *decision* must be enacted.

project

> A single set of *activities* with a stated objective, a definite end date and a definite set of deliverables. Project management is a specific approach distinct from the management of *business processes*.
>
> In *business process re-engineering*, projects are initiated for evaluating and developing new approaches to the business in the present or in the future, as part of an *improvement programme*. There are two types of improvement projects:
>
> 1) *business design projects* whose aim is to change significantly the scale/shape of the existing business or to take the organisation into new business areas.
>
> 2) *business improvement projects* whose aim is to make specific improvements, identified through the continuous quality assessment of *business processes* (usually as part of dealing with the issues generated when running already implemented processes).

quality

> The attributes of an end-product in complying with *customer requirements*.

relation

> In a *meta model*, an *entity type* can be connected to another through a relation.

role

> The position played in a process by an individual, team or unit. A given individual or team can play different roles. A role may be assumed by different people.

service

> The capability delivered to customers through the end-product. Service adds value in the customer process.
>
> *Examples: staff expertise, attitudes and behaviour, readiness to provide guidance, quality and appropriateness of guidance, ability to understand and meet customer needs, the manner in which customer requests are handled, consistency and integrity.*

strategic plan

> The document containing the *mission*, and *goals*, policies, the *values* and *strategy* of the organisation; usually limited to a given time scale (e.g. 'Five-Year Strategic Plan'). The preparation and production of the strategic plan is the role of the *Direction Management Process*. The strategic plan is the documentation of the mission and the direction of the organisation — of 'WHAT' it delivers, and of its *'raison d'être'*.

strategy

> The management approach chosen to pursue the *mission* and *goals* of the organisation according to its *values*; as captured in a *strategic plan*. There is only one strategy for the organisation, which sets the framework for the *change programme*.

tactical plan

> A plan for implementing the tactics over a chosen time scale, such as one or three years, contains a statement of the *objectives* and the required *capabilities* with quantitative attributes of benefits and business constraints — quality, cost and time scale (the 'WHEN').

tactics

> The management approach chosen by the organisation to acquire and manage the *capabilities* that it needs to meet its *objectives* — the 'HOW' of the organisation.

team contribution

> The result of the activity of a team towards the *objectives* of the organisation through the provision of a set of *competencies*.

type

> An *abstraction* which is used to describe the *entities* of our existing or imaginary worlds. Type has a generic set of known common characteristics and behaviour of its members, including features such as:

1) *singularity*: there is a 'oneness', a discrete, singular character allowing singular reference (naming) of individual members;

2) *distinctiveness*: members of the same type can be distinguished one from another;

3) *permanence*: the existence of a type is not dependent upon the existence of members (instances) of that type; an empty membership does not mean that the type has no existence as would be asserted in the set theory.

values

The set of desired behaviours and attitudes that the organisation uses to conduct business and the expected behaviour of the members of the organisation, consistent with its culture, and the expression of how the *strategy* is applied to pursue the *goals*. See also *ethical rules*.

Abbreviations and Acronyms

AFD	Activity Flow Diagram
BPR	Business Process Re-Engineering
CD	Concept Diagram
CSF	Critical Success Factor
ED	Event Diagram
EDI	Electronic Data Interchange
EQUITY™	trademark of London School of Economics
FOCUS-PDCA	Dr Deming's method: Find, Organise, Clarify and Understand - Plan, Do Check and Act (Walton 1990)
HIVIEW™	trademark of London School of Economics
IDEF	Integrated DEFinitions
Ithink®	trademark of High Performance Systems Inc.
KPI	Key Performance Indicator
MS-Windows™	trademark of Microsoft Inc.
OO	Object-Oriented approach
PRINCE	Project in Controlled Environment (© Crown copyright)
RAD	Role Activity Diagram
SADT™	Structured Analysis and Design Techniques, trademark of Softech Inc.
SSADM	Structured Systems Analysis and Design Method (© Crown copyright)
STD	State Transition Diagram
STELLA™	trademark of High Performance Systems Inc.
TAD	Team Architecture Diagram
TQM	Total Quality Management
VA	Value Analysis
VAD	Value-Added Diagram

Bibliography

In most of the following references, the ISBN number has been supplied for the convenience of the reader, but without responsibility for errors or omissions.

Adams B. (1987). *L'Analyse de la Valeur*, Entreprise Moderne d'Edition, Paris, ISBN 2.7101.0617.5.

Alexander C. (1979). *The Timeless Way of Building*, Oxford University Press, New York, ISBN 0.19.502402.8.

Beer S. (1966). *Decision and Control*, John Willey & Sons, Chichester, UK, ISBN 0.471.06210.3.

Beckett I. (1994). Private communication.

von Bertalanffy L. (1968). *General Systems Theory*, George Braziller, New York, ISBN 0.8076.0453.4.

Bradley K. (1993). *PRINCE: A Practical Handbook*, Butterworth-Heinemann, Oxford, ISBN 0.7506.0587.

Canavan P. (1994). *Dynamics of Growth on a Global Scale*, Annual Conference, Strategic Planning Society, 4 November, London.

Champy J. (1995). *Re-Engineering Management, the Mandate for New Leadership*, Harper Collins Pub., London, ISBN 0.00.255521.2.

Checkland P. and Scholes J. (1990). *Soft Systems Methodology in Action*, John Wiley & Sons, Chichester, UK, ISBN 0.471.92768.6.

Davis A.M. (1988). A Comparison of Techniques for the Specification of External System Behaviour, *Communications of the ACM*, Vol 31, no 9, pp 1098-1115, November 1988.

de Bono E. (1993). *Sur/Petition*, Harper Collins Pub., London, ISBN 0.002551.42.X.

Deming W.E. (1986). *Out of the Crisis*, Massachusetts Institute of Technology, Center for Advanced Engineering Study; Cambridge University Press, Cambridge, Mass.

Deming W.E. (1991). Deming Speaks to Senior Executives, *Booklet no. A10*, British Deming Association, Salisbury, UK, ISBN 1.873915.10.1.

Eden C. and Smithin T. (1984). *Cope User's Guide*, School of Management, University of Bath, UK.

Edwards J. (1984). *Process Architecture Design Technology (PTECH)*, internal reports, Associative Design Technology, Westborough, Mass.

Fisher R. & Ury W. (1991). *Getting to Yes*, Random Century Ltd, London, ISBN 0.7126.5528.X.

Forrester J.W. (1975). *Collected Papers of Jay W. Forrester*, Productivity Press, Cambridge, Mass.

Gilb T. (1976). *Software Metrics*, Chartwell-Bratt Ltd, Bromley, UK, ISBN091.44.12632.X.

Gilb T. (1988). *Principles of Software Engineering Management*, Addison-Wesley Pub. Co., Wokingham, UK, ISBN 0.210.19246.2.

van Griethuysen J.J. and King M.H eds (1985). *Assessment Guidelines for Conceptual Schema Language Proposals*, ISO TC97/SC21/WG5-3.

Guthrie E. (1994). *Re-Engineering the US Army*, presentation to The Strategic Planning Society, 10 October, London.

Hammer M. (1990). *Re-Engineering Work: Don't Automate — Obliterate, Harvard Business Review*, July-August, pp 104-112.

Hammer M. and Champy J. (1993). *Re-Engineering the Corporation, a Manifesto for Business Revolution*, Nicholas Brealey Publishing Ltd, London, ISBN 1.85788.029.3.

Handy C. (1994). *The Empty Raincoat*, Hutchinson, London, ISBN 0.09.178022.5.

Heskett J.L., Jone T.O., Loveman G.W., Sasser W.E Jr. and Schlesinger L.A. (1994). Putting the Service-Profit Chain to Work, *Harvard Business Review*, March-April, pp. 164-174,.

Humphrey W.S. (1989). *Managing the Software Process*, Addison Wesley Pub. Co., Reading Mass, reprinted 1990, ISBN 0.201.18095.2.

Hutton M.A. (1994). *The Management of Change, A Survey of UK Companies*, Proudfoot Creative Services Ltd, Richmond, UK.

IDEF (1992). IDEF 3 Process Description Capture Method Report, *Report AL-TR-1992-0057*, US Airforce System Command, Wright-Paterson Base, Ohio.

Jaques E. (1976). *A General Theory of Bureaucracy*, Heinemann Educational, London.

Jaques E., Gibson R.O & Isaac D.J. (1978). *Levels of Abstraction in Logic and Human Actions*, Heinemann Educational Books, London, ISBN 0.435.82280.2.

Kaplan R.S. and Norton D. (1992). Putting the Balanced Scorecard to Work, *Harvard Business Review*, September-October.

Kaplan R.S. and Norton D. (1993). The Balanced Scorecard Measures that Drive Performance, *Harvard Business Review*, January-February.

Krysalis Limited (1994a). *HIVIEW for Windows Starter Guide*, Krysalis Limited, Maidenhead, UK.

Krysalis Limited (1994b). *EQUITY for Windows Starter Guide*, Krysalis Limited, Maidenhead, UK.

Ling D.H.O. and Bell D.A. (1992). Modelling and Managing Time in Database Systems, *The Computer Journal*, Vol 35, no 4, pp 332-341, August 1992.

Martin J. and Odell J.J. (1992). *Object-Oriented Analysis and Design*, Prentice Hall Inc, Englewood Cliffs, New Jersey, ISBN 0.13.630245.9.

Meyer B. (1992). Design by Contract, in *Advances in Object-Oriented Software Engineering*, Prentice Hall International (UK) Ltd, Hemel Hempstead, ISBN 0.13.006578.1.

Miles L.D. (1972) *Techniques of Value Analysis and Engineering*, Mc Graw-Hill, New York.

Milne J. (1995). Survival of the Fittest, *Computing*, p. 49, 23 February.

Musashi M. (1982). *The Book of Five Rings*, Bantam Books, New York, ISBN 0.553.35170.2.

NCC (1990). *PRINCE: Structured Project Management*, NCC Blackwell Ltd, Oxford, ISBN 1.85554.012.6.

O'Brien D. and Wainwright J. (1993). Winning as Team of Teams - Transforming the Mindset of the Organisation at National & Provincial Building Society, *Business Change & Re-Engineering*, Vol 1, no 3, pp 19-25.

Odell, J. (1989). *Introduction to Object-Oriented Analysis, Concepts and Techniques*, James Odell Associates, Ann Arbor, Michigan, USA,

Ould M. A. (1993). *Process Modelling with RADs*, IOPener, Vol. 2, No. 1 & 2, August & December, Praxis plc, Bath.

Ould M.A.(1995). *Business Processes, Modelling and Analysis for Re-engineering and Improvement*, John Wiley & Sons, Chichester, UK, ISBN 0.471.95.353.0.

Partridge C. (1995). A Fistful of Smart Cards, *Computing*, p. 24-23 February 1995.

Pascale R.T. (1990). *Managing on the Edge*, Penguin Group, London (first published in the USA by Simon & Schuster), ISBN 0.14.014569.9.

Pellegrinelli S. and Bowman C. (1994). Implementing Strategy Through Projects, *Long Range Planning*, Vol 27, No 4, p. 125-132.

Peppard J. and Rowland P. (1995). *The Essence of Business Process Re-Engineering*, Prentice Hall International, Hemel Hempstead, UK, ISBN 0.13.310707.8.

Phillips, L.D. (1986). *Decision Analysis and its Application to Industry*, in Computer Assisted Decision Making, G. Mitra (Editor), Elsevier Science Pub, Amsterdam.

Phillips, L.D. (1989). *Decision Analysis in the 1990s*, Tutorial Papers in Operational Research, Ajran Shahani & Roy Stainton Eds, The Operational Research Society, Birmingham, UK.

Porter M.E. (1985). *Competitive Advantage: Creating and Sustaining Superior Performance*, The Free Press, New York.

Richmond B.M., Peterson S. & Vescuso P. (1987). *STELLA for Business*, Productivity Press, Cambridge, Mass.

Robinson P. ed. (1992). HOOD Reference Manual Issue 3.0, *Object-Oriented Design*, Chapman & Hall, London, ISBN 0.412.40520.2 (UK); ISBN 0.442.31411.6 (USA).

Russell B. (1956). *Mathematical Logic as based on the Theory of Types*, reproduced in *Logic and Knowledge*, Unwin Hayman, London, ISBN 0.04.440260.0.

Sadler P. (1994). *Designing Organisations: The Foundation for Excellence*, Kogan Page, London, ISBN 0.7494.1394.8.

Spencer L.M. and Spencer S.M. (1993). *Competence at Work, Models for Superior Performance*, John Wiley & Sons, New York, ISBN 0.471.54809.X.

Stalk G., Evans P. & Shalman L.E. (1992). Competing on Capabilities: The New Rules of Corporate Strategy, *Harvard Business Review*, March-April, p.57-69,.

Tayson C. (1994). *Re-Engineering the Future, Proceedings of BPR 94 Conference*, Business Intelligence Limited, London, 26-27 October.

Thomas L.C. (1984). *Games, Theory and Applications*, John Wiley & Sons, Chichester. UK.

Tijou F. (1994). *Selecting an Approach to Developing Competence and Managing Performance*, paper presented at the Institute of Directors, Management Competency Development Ltd, London.

Toffler A. (1970). *Future Shock*, Bantam Books Inc., New York, ISBN 0.553.13264.4.

Toffler A. (1980). *The Third Wave*, Pan Books Ltd, London, ISBN 0.330.26337.4.

Veasey P. (1993). 'Experiences in Process Mapping', *IOPT Club Seminar*, London, 2 November 1993.

Walton M. (1990). *Deming Management at Work*, G.P. Putnam Sons.

Whitehead A.N. and Russell B. (1910). *Principia Mathematica*, Cambridge University Press, Cambridge, UK, ISBN 0.521.09187.X.

Zimmermann H.J., Zadeh L.A. and Gaines B.R. (1984). *Fuzzy Sets and Decision Analysis*, North-Holland, Amsterdam, Holland, ISBN 0.444.86593.4.

FURTHER READING ON DECISION ANALYSIS

Buchanan J.T. (1982). *Discrete and Dynamic Decision Analysis*, John Wiley & Sons, Chichester, UK.

Howard R.A. and Matheson J.F. (1984). *The Principles and Applications of Decision Analysis*, Strategic Decision Group, Menlo Park, California.

Mallen G.L. (1970). Control Theory and Decision Making in Organisations, *Measurement and Control*, Vol 3, March 1970, pp T46-T48.

Raiffa H. (1968). *Decision Analysis*, Addison-Wesley, Reading, Mass.

SELECTED READING ON PROCESS DESIGN

The following is a personal selection of some of the books recently published in Business Process Re-engineering and related cultural issues; some of them have already been quoted in the main text.

James Champy, (1995). *Re-engineering Management*, Harper Collins Publishers Ltd, London, ISBN 0.00.255521.2.

The state of the BPR revolution (not altogether brilliant) after the initial 'Re-engineering the Corporation' manifesto and an update on actual projects in the industry.

P. Davenport (1993). *Process Innovation, Re-engineering Work through IT*, Havard Business School, Cambridge, Mass.

Comprehensive description of an approach to BPR, with emphasis on the role of IT.

Deming W.E. (1986). *Out of the Crisis*, Massachusetts Institute of Technology, Center for Advanced Engineering Study; Cambridge University Press, Cambridge, Mass., and

Walton M. (1990). *Deming Management at Work*, G.P. Putnam & Sons.

These two books form the core exposition of Dr Deming's approach to management, acknowledged as the major factor of the Japanese success after the war. The philosophy which has guided the creation of this book is totally compatible with Dr Deming's approach.

Eliyahu M. Goldratt & Jeff Cox (1984). *The Goal, A Process of Ongoing Improvement*, Gower Pub. Ltd, Aldershot, UK also USA version North River Press, Inc., 1984 and 1986

Eliyahu M. Goldratt (1994). *It's not Luck*, Gower Pub. Ltd, Aldershot, UK, ISBN 0.566.07637.3

The fictional story of a manager coping with change, improvement and corporate re-engineering. In *The Goal*, he is a manufacturing plant manager and in *It's not Luck*, he is promoted to the board. Puts the human dimension to a rather abstract subject.

Michael Hammer & James Champy. (UK print 1993). *Re-engineering the Corporation,* Nicholas Brealey Pub. Ltd, London, ISBN 1-85788-029-3.

> The seminal book, expanding on the original article published in the *Harvard Business Journal,* passionate preaching of the BPR belief.

Charles Handy, (1990, First published 1989). *The Age of Unreason,* Arrow Books Ltd, London, ISBN 0.09.975740.0.

> Powerful series of essays on the change in the culture of society and organisations during the 1980s and 1990s.

Charles Handy (1992, First published 1978). *Gods of Management,* Century Business, London, ISBN 0.7126.5142.X.

> An original approach to understanding different styles of management.

Charles Handy (1993, First published 1976). *Understanding Organisations,* Penguin Books, London, ISBN 0-14-015603-8.

> Another thought-provoking essay by Charles Handy on how management works in practice.

Nick Obolensky (1994). *Practical Business Re-Engineering,* Kogan Page Ltd, London, ISBN 0.7494.1408.1.

> A method and an inventory of techniques relevant to process design with eleven case studies including European experience.

Pascale R.T. (1990). *Managing on the Edge,* Penguin Group, London (first published in the USA by Simon & Schuster), ISBN 0.14.014569.9.

> An analysis of some of the underlying principles of modern management through a number of case studies, by one of the better articulated gurus of management. Much material drawn from consulting work to American Corporations.

Peppard J. and Rowland P. (1995). *The Essence of Business Process Re-Engineering,* Prentice Hall International, Hemel Hempstead, UK, ISBN 0.13.310707.8.

> A good inventory of techniques relevant to process design and process improvements. Many references.

Philip Sadler (1994). *Designing Organizations, the Foundation for Excellence,* Kogan Page Ltd, London, ISBN 0.7494.1394.8.

> Focuses on the organisation as a social system, the organisation as a framework for the relationship between people.

Michael S. Scott Morton (1991). *The Corporation of the 1990s,* Oxford University Press, Oxford.

> One of the deeper works on the subject of BPR by an established consultant on management matters. Looks at the subject from a management angle, the emphasis is not on how to do it.

Don Tapscott & Art Caston (1993). *Paradigm Shift*, McGraw-Hill Inc., ISBN 0 07 062857 2.

    Analysis of the opportunities offered by IT in shaping more effective organisations.

Index